International
Relations
under Risk

International Relations under Risk

Framing State Choice

Jeffrey D. Berejikian

State University of New York Press

Published by
State University of New York Press, Albany

For information, address State University of New York Press,
90 State Street, Suite 700, Albany, NY 12207

Production by Michael Haggett
Marketing by Jennifer Giovani

Library of Congress Cataloging in Publication Data

Berejikian, Jeffrey D., 1965–
    International relations under risk : framing state choices / Jeffrey D. Berejikian.
        p. cm. — (SUNY series in global politics)
    Includes bibliographical references and index.
    ISBN 0-7914-6007-X (alk. paper) — ISBN 0-7914-6008-8 (pbk. : alk. paper)
    1. International relations—Decision making. 2. International relations—Psycholog-
ical aspects. I. Title. II. Series.

JZ1253.B47 2004
327.1′01′9—dc22
                                                               2003070447

10 9 8 7 6 5 4 3 2 1

*to my parents Harry and Alice,
with love, admiration and friendship.*

Contents

List of Figures

Preface and Acknowledgments

Ultimately, the study of human political behavior, both individual and aggregate, can only be understood as a function of deliberate choices. Sometimes, the list of available choices is severely constrained such that people don't have much or any freedom in the matter. Often, the result is different than intended. But if *something* happens, it is because someone or some group made a *choice*. A simple yet undeniable truth, it took considerable effort from both of my academic advisors at the University of Oregon, John Dryzek and John Orbell, to bring me to it.

There is currently a lively and interesting debate about the cognitive mechanisms driving the choices that individuals make. The purpose of this book is to demonstrate that both the study of international relations and the discipline of political science have much to gain by paying greater attention to that discussion. The pressure from cognitive psychology and related fields on political science is increasing, and cognitive principles will continue to force their way into our models. I hope here to add a bit of speed to a process that is already well under way.

I am indebted to many colleagues. Foremost, I thank Dryzek and Orbell who, each in a different fashion, nurtured my interest in the study of politics and patiently redirected me when I ran astray with ideas while in graduate school. But for their efforts, I'd not have begun the intellectual journey that produced this book. Michael Huelshoff, Lars Skalnes, and Ronald Mitchell each helped in sharpening portions of the argument in its early form. Jess Morrisette has been an invaluable guide as the project neared completion. The editors at SUNY Press, and the anonymous reviewers for the manuscript

Reprinted by permission of Cambridge University Press from Jeffrey D. Berejikian, "The Gains Debate: Framing State Choice," *American Political Science Review*, Vol. 91, No. 4 (1997), and by permission of Sage Publications Ltd., from Jeffrey D. Berejikian, "A Cognitive Theory of Deterrence," *Journal of Peace Research*, Vol. 39, no. 2 (2002).

provided incisive criticism and guidance. Portions of chapters 5 and 6 appeared previously in the *American Political Science Review*, portions of chapter 3 appeared previously in *Journal of Peace Research*. The comments from editors and anonymous referees at these journals considerably improved the analysis in those chapters.

Finally, the support, encouragement, and partnership of Holly Marie Berejikian sustained me throughout this project. It continues to do so.

Chapter 1

Competing Models
of Decision Making

INTRODUCTION

Few decision-making environments are fraught with greater risk than the
anarchy of the international system. Mistaken foreign policy holds the potential for disaster, and is alone justification for the enormous time spent by students of international politics on foreign policy choice. Traditionally, scholars
have assumed that leaders deploy rational decision rules in pursuit of state
goals. However, accumulating empirical evidence from laboratory experimentation suggests that individuals systematically violate the behavioral expectations of rationality. As a result, while many still defend the assumption of
rationality as the proper starting point for the scientific examination of interstate behavior, there is also a growing call for new models of international politics based upon the actual capacities of decision makers.

Just as anarchy places state survival at risk, the empirical findings from
cognitive psychology similarly threaten traditional international relations
theory. Research demonstrates that human choice is as much a result of consistent heuristics and biases as it is a function of calculated costs and benefits.[1]
Prospect theory is one branch of this larger cognitive psychological investigation into the structure of human choice. Indeed, it is the prominent finding
and currently stands as the "leading alternative to expected utility as a theory
of choice under conditions of risk" (Levy 1996, 179). In direct contrast to the
predictions of rational choice, prospect theory finds that decision makers do
not maximize objective outcomes. Instead, individuals consistently overweight

losses relative to gains and are risk averse when confronted with choices between gains while risk acceptant when confronted with losses.

The fact that actual decision makers choose as the research on prospect theory suggests and not as our theories of international politics assume, while increasingly recognized, has not yet forced a thorough reconsideration of core theoretical propositions in the field. The purpose behind this book is to begin such a review by offering a new set of theoretical propositions about international politics securely anchored to empirical research in cognitive psychology.

Support for such an approach is growing. Its wellspring is the realization that rationalist theory does not capture well the actual behavior of actors making political choices. This view has now penetrated into the heart of the discipline. For example, Elinor Ostrom's presidential address to the American Political Science Association (1998) challenged political science to develop a behavioral theory of collective action. Theories of politics, according to Ostrom, should be "based on models of the individual consistent with empirical evidence about how individuals make decisions in social-dilemma situations" (1). The application of cognitive principles to the study of international politics is consistent with Ostrom's general call to the discipline of political science. The most productive theories of politics will be those securely anchored to the actual characteristics of human choice.

Ultimately, social science aspires to be relevant. In political science, the belief that we knew too little about the mechanisms of political choice to offer useful counsel to policymakers was largely responsible for the field's alienation from actual political practice. For many in the discipline, this suggested the need to step back and systematize the examination of politics under the framework of science, study the social world, and then return to political leaders with a report of findings. Proponents of rational choice theory continue to argue that their approach promises the best chance of producing the kind of disciplinary consensus enjoyed, for example, by economics. As with economic behavior, they maintain that rational choice is therefore the most efficient path to accumulating useful knowledge about political behavior because rationality assumptions easily and efficiently lend themselves to the construction of deductive and testable theory.[2]

However, the field from which rational models were imported to political science is itself rapidly changing. In consecutive years (2001, 2002), the Nobel Prize for economics has gone to individuals for their work in behavioral economics. George Akerlof received the award by demonstrating that "if there is any subject in economics which should be behavioral, it is macroeconmics" (Akerlof 2002, 427–428). Daniel Kahneman helped conceive the field of behavioral decision theory which now stands as an empirically grounded alternative to standard rationalist assumptions.[3] Behavioral economists are no less committed to the scientific study of economic behavior than their traditional counterparts. Indeed, their purpose is to develop models firmly grounded in the actual capacities of human decision making, thus improving our understanding of economic behavior.

The comparative strength of rational choice over psychological approaches as a tool for international analysis has long been its utility in the construction of an elaborate and sophisticated set of interrelated theoretical propositions about the dynamics of international relations that enjoy considerable empirical support. These include but are not limited to deterrence, bargaining, cooperation, economic behavior, and the deployment of power. By contrast, psychological explanations have not generated a similarly integrated set of theorems about international politics that might rival rational choice. While a considerable body of research on prospect theory outside political science exists, scholars studying international politics have only recently taken it up. Attempts to resolve the so-called "cognitive-rational debate" in international relations scholarship are therefore premature (e.g., Geva and Minz 1997). Proponents of rational choice can correctly proclaim the approach superior simply because no viable alternative exists (e.g., Morrow 1997).

None of this implies that all rational models are incorrect. It does suggest, however, that contemporary cognitive psychology can also serve as the cornerstone for the systematic examination of political behavior. Stated directly, we now know enough about the actual process of decision making to attempt theories of international politics based upon the real capacities of decision makers. Indeed, the limited but growing body of research using prospect theory to explain state behavior already describes the nascent contours of an alternative cognitive framework. The motivation for this study is to build upon these existing insights and construct a new set of interconnected propositions organized around prospect theory so that a systematic comparison of the two perspectives becomes possible. This is a first step: no single book could stand as a complete substitute for the impressive set of propositions already constructed under rational choice. Instead, the intent is to demonstrate that it is possible, with an empirically established model of decision making, to connect the various subfields of international relations in a way similar to that now standing as the highest achievement of rationalist theory.

COGNITION AND INTERNATIONAL RELATIONS THEORY

Previous psychological explanations for state behavior often relied upon the personality traits of decision makers, upon the information flows unique to the decision set, or upon a unique group dynamic in the decision setting. Despite attempts to introduce deductive rigor to psychological studies, many continue to rely heavily upon these or similar contextually unique variables.[4] Rational choice thus enjoys a considerable advantage in terms of its capacity to produce deductive explanations. Similarly, contemporary developments in constructivist theory focus upon the socially constituted identity and interests of states. Such efforts often lack an adequate theory of human agency, frequently reducing actors entirely to their social milieu (Checkel 1998).[5] Rational choice, firmly grounded in human agency, is thus better positioned to produce theories that provide policymakers with useful guidelines for making intelligent choices in a strategic environment.

Importantly, many of these past deficiencies no longer apply to contemporary cognitive models. The promise of prospect theory lies in the fact that it permits the construction of deductive theory while maintaining a clear focus on human agency. It thus co-opts the primary benefit of rational models while genuinely depicting the process of human choice.

However, the degree to which prospect theory penetrates into the mainstream of international relations theory will rest upon its empirical power. Ultimately, a portion of the ideas developed here may fail to hold up under empirical scrutiny. Nonetheless, the possibility that some of the logical paths that prospect theory may take us down will lead to empirical dead ends is not a reason to stop exploring. At this point, we do not know how many paths there are, let alone which ones will prove most fruitful. Judgments about the utility of prospect theory are therefore impossible without first systematically exploring what the framework has to say about the practice of international relations. By developing the theoretical implications of prospect theory, students of international politics will be able to select those most likely to produce important empirical insights.

Given the number of extensions and modifications to classic rationality, it is best depicted as a family of theories rather than a single unified model of choice (Schoemaker 1982). The definition of rationality used here is that of classic expected utility theory, first developed by von Neumann and Morgenstern, wherein actors evaluate alternatives and select a maximizing strategy (von Neumann and Morgenstern 1947). Prospect theory is similar to rational choice in that decisions involve calculation and are goal oriented. It is therefore distinct from irrational decision making. By "irrational" I mean making decisions based upon, for example, astrology, good-luck charms, habit, and other mechanisms that clearly provide little or no useful information to the decision maker (Dawes 1988, chap. 1). Because decisions under prospect theory are structured, stable, and predictable, there is a tendency to view it simply as an extension of rational choice. However, such a characterization undermines an essential difference between the two approaches. As we shall see, under prospect theory individuals often do not maximize objective outcomes, even with perfect information.

The central role of classic rationality in contemporary international relations is obvious. It is the explicit model of choice in theories like modern realism, deterrence politics, collective action, political economy, and foreign policy. True rationality, however, is often beyond the capacity of actual decision makers. Time constraints, huge amounts of information, and uncertainty, combined with cognitive limitations, make it simply impossible for foreign policy actors to select a universally maximizing choice. One common response to this challenge is to argue that classic rationality can be replaced with a "satisficing" or "bounded" conception that more accurately depicts actual decision making while retaining the principal benefits of conventional rational choice models—namely their parsimony and predictive breadth. However, scholars in international relations have not energetically embraced this position. Surprisingly little research deliberately adopts a cognitively limited view of decision makers, and the explicit and implicit use of classic rationality by far outweighs that which does exist.

Instead, the field gravitated to a second position. All theories are abstractions from a complex reality. What is important is not the truth of the assumptions embedded in the theory but the predictive power of the resultant model (e.g., Waltz 1990). However, the presumed predictive power of rational choice explanations is itself increasingly questioned. Herbert Simon first noted that much of the explanatory work of rational models comes not from the "Herculean" assumption that people strictly maximize, but from a rich set of auxiliary claims about what people want and how they view the world (Simon 1983). Explanation comes from the detailed contextual data that accompany rational analysis, not from the assumption of rationality itself. Jervis (1978), in a review of early game theoretic applications to interstate behavior, concludes similarly. Emphasizing rationality in the construction of international relations theory draws our attention "away from the areas that contain much of the explanatory 'action' in which we are interested" (325).

The challenge posed by contemporary cognitive models is even more fundamental. Behavioral models of choice—like prospect theory—illustrate why it is impractical to expect that testing hypotheses derived from theories whose fundamental assumptions we know to be false will advance our understanding of political behavior. Simply stated, prediction and understanding are not the same. An imaginary farmer in pre-Copernican times could do quite well in predicting the timing of the sunrise and sunset, as well as the seasons, all from a view of the solar system that had the sun revolving around the earth. The farmer's model of the solar system would be predictive, but it would also be incorrect. More importantly, much would be concealed from the farmer, and this model is really only predictive in the narrowest sense. It tells us nothing about the actual relationship between planets in the solar system, and thus it would be useless for more complicated tasks like sending a rocket to the moon. The analogy hits close to its mark in the field of behavioral economics, where many now understand that "the uniformities in human choice behavior which lie behind market behavior may result from principles which are of a completely different sort from those generally accepted" (Grether and Plott, 1979, 623).

For scholars in the field of international relations, the challenge of cognitive psychology is similar. Rather than debate whether or not a particular assumption is useful for theory construction, we should ask ourselves if it still makes sense to continue with models that often contain known and mistaken representations about real-world actors. The issue becomes more compelling given that we have at our disposal models from cognitive psychology that are in fact accurate descriptions of the actual process of decision making.

Prospect Theory

As noted above, early psychological approaches positioned themselves as alternatives to rational choice in order to offer a more accurate portrayal of real-world decision making. However, these descriptively rich models were heavily dependent upon contextual factors, complicating the construction of deductive theory. Outside political science, scholars studying decision making also concluded that the assumption of rationality could not be reconciled with mounting empirical evidence about actual human choice and developed prospect theory as an alternative.[6] Results under prospect theory demonstrate that individuals systematically violate the prescriptions of classic rationality, and this places two pillars of rational choice in dispute. First, individuals assess the desirability of prospects against a reference point, rather than against their net asset position. Second, actors do not treat choices between gains and losses identically.

Prospect theory builds upon the observation that individuals evaluate choices against a value function with specific characteristics. First, individuals experience diminishing sensitivity to increasing gains or losses. For example, an initial windfall of $1,000 is more highly valued than is the same $1,000 when added on top of an initial gain of $10,000. Second, the value function for losses is steeper than for gains, as individuals feel the sting of loss more acutely than an equivalent gain. This steeper losses curve reflects the "observation that a loss has a greater subjective effect than an equivalent gain" (Kahneman and Tversky 1982, 166). Finally, decision makers evaluate each choice anew and against a neutral reference point. Combined, these characteristics suggest decision makers evaluate outcomes using two value functions—one for gains and one for losses—rather than a single utility function as proposed under conventional rational choice.

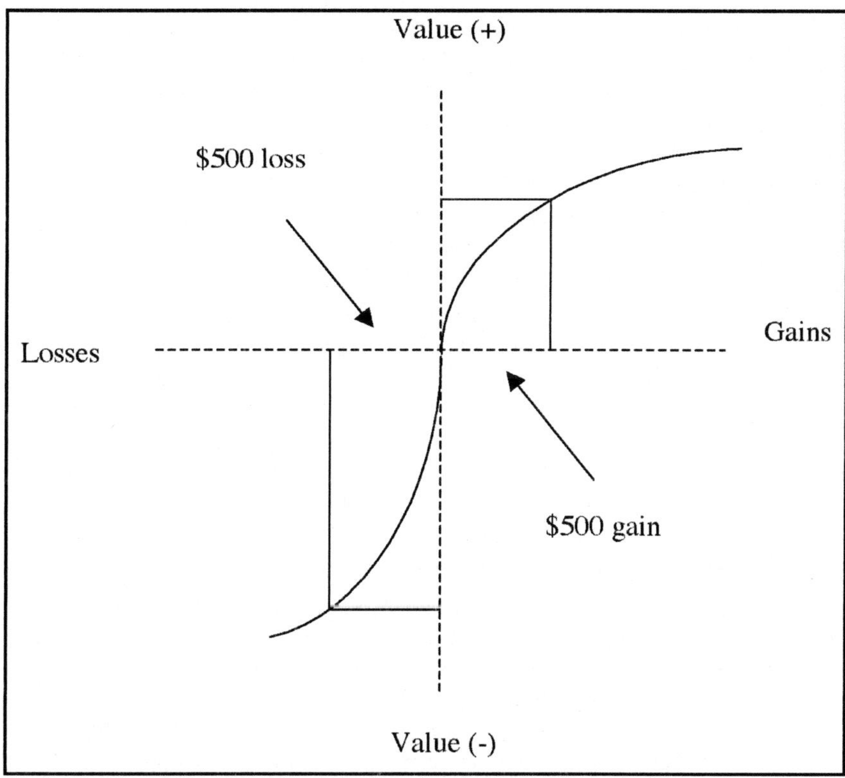

FIGURE 1.1. Example s-shaped value function under prospect theory.

Figure 1.1 describes these functions. Here, the graph's origin represents the reference point for evaluating prospects as gains or losses. Most often, this reference point represents status quo conditions, though this is not theoretically necessary.[7] The s-shaped form of the value function also captures the diminishing relationship between objective gains or losses with subjective value. A central distinction between prospect theory and rational choice lies in this asymmetrical relationship between gains and losses. Expected utility theory holds that decision makers appraise the desirability of outcomes against their net asset position, and therefore that they evaluate both gains and losses against a single utility function. This is not true under prospect theory. Notice also that the function for losses is steeper than for gains, reflecting the observation that losses hurt more than gains feel good.

Prospect theory also distinguishes two stages in the decision-making process. The first is editing, in which decision makers assess outcomes and place them in a gains or losses frame. The second stage involves an evaluation of prospects, wherein individuals select the prospect of the highest value.[8] The initial editing stage is crucial under prospect theory because it powerfully influences the subsequent evaluation of outcomes. The importance of this influence can be illustrated by example (Tversky and Kahneman 1981, 453). Imagine the outbreak of a disease that, if left untreated, is expected to kill 600 people. Consider two possible abatement strategies.

Strategy 1:

Program A: 200 people will be saved.
Program B: 1/3 probability that 600 people will be saved;
2/3 probability that no one will be saved.

Strategy 2

Program C: 400 people will die.
Program D: 1/3 probability that no one will die;
2/3 probability that 600 people will die.

The two choice sets are identical. In each, the certain prospect saves 200 people from the disease, while the gamble contains an expected outcome of 400 deaths. The only difference is that the language in the first set of strategies describes the choices in terms of the number of lives saved, while the second set describes the same choices in terms of the number of lives lost. Nonetheless, this difference in the frame systematically influences individual assessments about which strategy is desirable.[9] Results show that the majority of individuals consistently choose Program A in the first problem set, but opt for Program D in the second. The finding is quite robust. Studies deliberately designed to refute it have reconfirmed the basic result (Grether and Plott 1979). Subsequent research has also confirmed these findings outside the laboratory in a wide variety of real-world settings.[10]

Such preference reversal violates the principle of invariance central to classic rationality. Variations in the form of presentation that have no impact upon actual outcomes should not affect one's preferences. Different presentations of the same problem should produce the same choice. Note also that these findings break with the rational model in that the decisional determinant is not the expected outcome. It is instead how actors perceived their options relative to the status quo. Indeed, in an important sense, objective outcomes become unimportant because "the same decision can be framed in several different ways and different frames lead to different decisions" (Kahneman and Tversky 1982, 165).

Prospect theory thus finds that individuals tend to be risk averse—defined as a preference for a riskless prospect over a gamble of equal or greater value—in the domain of gains and risk acceptant—defined as a preference for a

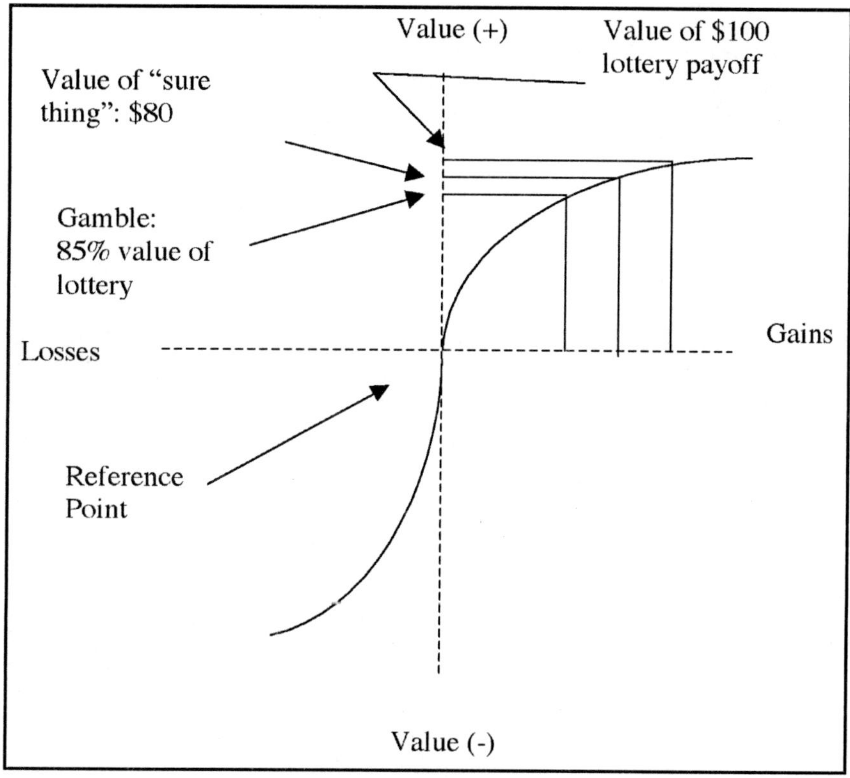

FIGURE 1.2. Example lottery imposed over s-shaped
value function under prospect theory

gamble over a riskless prospect of equal or greater value—in the domain of
losses. This means that individuals often "forgo the option that offers the highest monetary expectation" (Kahneman and Tversky 1982, 160). Actors do not
maximize objective outcomes. Figure 1.2 plots a set of gains and losses for a
hypothetical lottery over the s-shaped function. In the gains quadrant, an individual would prefer a sure gain of $80 to an 85 percent chance to win $100. In
the losses quadrant, the same individual would prefer a gamble offering an 85
percent chance of losing $100 to a certain loss of $80.

Finally, notice that the value function for losses is steeper than for gains.
In figure 1.1, the subjective pain of a $500 loss is greater than the benefit of an
equal $500 gain. The result of this is loss aversion, wherein actors pursue costly
strategies intended to avoid loss beyond a rational expectation of benefits. This
finding is consistent with an observed endowment effect, which "enhances not

the desirability of what one owns, but the pain of forsaking it" (Nincic 1997, 99). The clear tendency here is to place a greater value on that already possessed compared to equivalent goods not yet acquired.

ASSESSMENT

Prospect theory models the subjectivity of actual human choice. The important point here is that our theories of international relations lag behind our knowledge of human decision making. For example, current models of military deterrence simply do not acknowledge risk-acceptant nonmaximizing behavior, despite the fact that this is sometimes how decision makers act. Given modern military technology, the importance of accurately predicting such choices is obvious. Under prospect theory, the deployment of deterrence threats can have several unintended consequences not predicted by rational choice. Credible threats might generate a losses frame for the target government, pushing it into risky behavior. Such behavior might include abandoning negotiations when the threatening state was simply attempting to secure a better deal. Similarly, certain deterrence threats may induce risk-acceptant aggression even when there is a low probability of success. This is exactly the sort of behavior that deterrence is designed to stop. The implications of loss aversion are also compelling. For example, from a rationalist perspective, it distorts subjective assessments attached to the value of concessions demanded by an adversary in negotiations, making cooperation more difficult than traditional theory predicts (Kristensen 1997). Loss aversion affects market transactions, resulting in so-called market sickness whereby social welfare is reduced (Borges 1998). All of this will be explored in detail later. The point here is that our understanding of decision making under risk is quite different with prospect theory as the model of state choice.

The ability of rational choice theory to pull together disparate aspects of international politics into a coherent whole lies in the assertion of a universal state decision rule, one that produces consistent and stable choice across space and time. If prospect theory is to stand as an alternative to rationality, it must also assert its viability across contexts. The empirical research conducted thus far suggests that this is the case. In the laboratory, the predictions under prospect theory manifest in an array of choice problems, ranging from the selection of alternative public policies to the decision to purchase a lottery ticket. Outside the laboratory, studies find support in the decisions of individuals considering everything from purchasing flood insurance to supporting military intervention.

While its behavioral expectations differ from rational choice, decisions under prospect theory remain stable and predictable. Deviations from rationality are not trivial exceptions but are themselves important phenomena for which an explanation is possible. It remains an open question as to whether prospect theory holds the potential for an independent framework for state behavior that is superior, supplementary, or inferior to existing rational choice theory. The issue cannot be resolved until scholars systematically compare the two approaches. The first step toward this end is to integrate prospect theory into some of the existing frameworks in the study of international politics, and contrast the results against those that already exist under rational choice.

There are then several tasks for this book. The first is to pull together some of the existing research in the study of international politics that utilizes prospect theory. This establishes the usefulness of the approach and lays the foundation for the subsequent analysis of contemporary international relations theory. The second task is to suggest new applications for prospect theory. This is my primary purpose, and it will involve both revisiting extant theories as well as developing new models of state behavior. Some bodies of rationalist theory remain unaffected by the introduction of prospect theory, others require modest revision, and others still require a compete reworking. Such an analysis cannot be exhaustive. Still, the range of subjects covered in the following chapters is enough to support the contention that prospect theory represents a viable alternative for theory construction in international politics. Because the purpose here is comparison, the analysis highlights the differences between the two perspectives. The theories selected for discussion are those that produce sharp contrasts between prospect theory and rational choice, while the bodies of theory in which prospect theory and rational choice predict the same behavior are de-emphasized. A third task is to conduct an initial empirical assessment of the new frameworks produced by prospect theory. The case for a cognitive research program is strengthened by the degree to which the new models made possible by prospect theory themselves produce better explanations of state behavior. The evidence from the Montreal Protocol presented in chapters 6 and 7 establishes that many of the propositions developed under prospect theory enjoy empirical support.

CHAPTER SUMMARY

Chapter 2 explores several of the logical and methodological issues that emerge with the adoption of prospect theory as a cornerstone for political analysis. While at first glance there appear to be significant hurdles to constructing an integrated cognitive framework, these concerns are in fact empirical questions that will be resolved as research progresses. I then offer a selective discussion of the growing body of existing research that deploys prospect theory in an analysis of international politics. The review demonstrates that prospect theory has made an initial contribution to international relations theory by opening a new set of important theoretical and empirical concerns. The next step in the cognitive enterprise is to construct a set of interconnected propositions about international politics, much like that which already exists under rational choice.

The following three chapters attempt to refashion traditional international relations theory and unfold roughly in the same way. Each chapter initially presents the logic and behavioral expectations of a rational model, with special attention placed upon that aspect to which I think prospect theory might apply. Each then modifies or extends the analysis by integrating prospect theory. Finally, the significance of such modifications is assessed.

Chapter 3 reanalyzes power. Most importantly, prospect theory permits a new definition for the use of power: power as the manipulation of the decisional frame. The deployment of power, because it can alter the decision frame in the target state, often produces unintended consequences that do not reveal themselves under rational choice. Among these is that the application of threats predictably produces unwanted changes in target behavior. Traditional theories suggest that states confronted with power alter their preferences by scaling back their goals (for example, less territory or smaller economic gains). Prospect theory goes beyond this to demonstrate that states do not just scale back existing goals, but that, when confronted by power, states may also adopt new goals and strategies that are not predicted by rational choice. Consequently, rational choice and prospect theory disagree over the kind of military and economic threats that are likely to be productive and those that are likely fail.

Chapter 4 focuses upon interstate cooperation. It combines prospect theory with existing concepts from game theory and collective action to present an integrated framework for collaborative behavior that stands in contrast to the predictions of rational choice. Specifically, states in a gains frame will decline cooperation even when the expected outcome is greater than noncooperation, so long as cooperation also carries with it some risk of loss. By contrast, states in a losses frame will cooperate even when the expected losses from cooperation are greater than noncooperation, so long as cooperation also provides some small chance of improvement. Prospect theory suggests then that cooperation is both easier and more difficult than rational choice predicts.

Chapter 5 explores the constitution of state goals. Rational choice treats preferences as exogenous—a tradition followed in most international relations theory. This chapter takes up the task of explaining goals themselves, so that models of state behavior treat preferences endogenously. One result of the deployment of rational choice was the devolution of theory into competing camps. This bifurcation is a direct cause of the "gains debate" between realists and liberals that occupied much attention during the 1990s. The debate was largely a theoretical artifact, deriving from a particular application of rational choice and ultimately subsided without a satisfactory resolution. After a brief discussion of the origins of the debate, a resolution grounded in prospect theory is developed and discussed. Prospect theory not only accurately describes the strategies used by governments to secure realist and liberal goals; it also sheds light on the origins of the goals themselves. In addition, the new framework avoids the common pitfall, best exemplified in the gains debate, of developing unnecessarily antagonistic theoretical frameworks for understanding international politics.

Chapters 6 and 7 offer an initial empirical investigation of some of the models produced by prospect theory. These chapters examine the Montreal Protocol, a landmark environmental agreement designed to ban the production and use of CFCs in order to save the earth's protective ozone layer. As an initial probe, some of the propositions developed in previous chapters will remain unexamined in the Montreal case. Still, the nature of these negotiations permits simultaneous investigation into several of the propositions developed here, including the role of power and threats in chapter 3, the conditions conducive to cooperation discussed in chapter 4, and the changing nature of state goals discussed in chapter 5.

Chapter 6 explores the behavior of the European Community. Consistent with the argument developed in earlier chapters, it was not until the onset of a losses frame that the EC gambled on a negotiated settlement and attempted to secure advantages in relative position through cooperation. Prior to the negotiations, the EC enjoyed both relative and absolute gains in the production and sale of CFCs. Realism predicts that EC policy would attempt to protect recent relative gains in the international CFC trade and solidify its newfound position as the dominant international supplier to the global market. Liberalism predicts protection of absolute gains in the form of recently increased production levels. While these are not necessarily exclusive goals, the EC was not able to pursue them simultaneously. We would expect therefore a consistent policy from the EC—that it would choose either absolute gains or relative position. However, EC policy was not consistent and instead shifted from protection of production levels to the pursuit of relative gains. Prospect theory predicts these changes in policy by establishing first that the decision frame for the EC switched from gains to losses, and second that with this change in the frame EC policy shifted from absolute gains pursuit and risk avoidance to relative gains pursuit and risk acceptance.

Chapter 7 examines U.S. participation in the Montreal Protocol. The analysis first documents the U.S. decision to ban unilaterally CFC aerosol propellants. Initially the issue lacked a decision frame, as U.S. policymakers possessed a technical rather than economic definition of the problem. During this period, the United States blocked efforts to complete an international treaty. With the emergence of a losses frame for ozone politics in the United States, decision makers adopted a new strategy and American policy breaks sharply to embrace risk acceptance, cooperation, and relative gains pursuit. A key aspect distinguishing U.S. and European behavior is the different political process that ultimately defined the decision frame in each case. Changes in the international political topography imposed a new frame upon the member states of the European Community. Such changes were thus external to the EC, originating in the international system. For the United States, shifting domestic coalitions in the political debate over an appropriate regulatory response to ozone depletion was primarily responsible for the creation of a decision frame.

Chapter 8 concludes the analysis of the Montreal Protocol and suggests that prospect theory meets the challenge placed before it by rational choice. Specifically, it is possible to connect the various subfields of international relations with an empirically established model of decision making in a way similar to that standing in international relations theory as the highest achievement of rational choice. Additionally, as chapters 6 and 7 demonstrate, prospect theory also possesses considerable potential to shed empirical light on heretofore puzzling state behavior. Finally, I offer some comments on expanding this approach to international relations by integrating additional findings from cognitive psychology into the framework offered here.

Chapter 2

Prospect Theory and International Relations

Introduction

This chapter reviews the objections to using prospect theory in building models of state behavior and finds that none of them ultimately prove crippling. Prospect theory thus stands as a viable alternative for theory construction in the study of international politics. A selective discussion of research using prospect theory is then presented. This scholarship is successful in demonstrating prospect theory's implications for understanding discrete foreign policy choices, but it has yet to develop an integrated set of deductive propositions comparable to rationalist theory.

Arguments against Prospect Theory

The Imperatives of Anarchy

Perhaps the most compelling theoretical challenge to using prospect theory in the study of international politics originates with standard economic theory. In a competitive market, the competition between firms for profit positions rivals to capitalize upon bad choices, thereby forcing all firms to eliminate nonmaximizing behavior and to adopt rational decision rules. This commitment is the standard response from economics to the challenge posed by cognitive psychology (Friedman 1953). The argument becomes relevant for students of international politics through neorealism. Waltz (1979), for example, argues that the competition for power in the international system is analogous to the struggle for profit by firms in a free market. The unforgiving logic of the international market for power will punish those states that do not make maximizing choices about their security. The result is that nonrational behavior like that uncovered by prospect theory, if consistently observed, would lead states to ruin.

The main objection to this "market negation thesis" is that it applies only in perfect or near-perfect markets. Monopolistic or oligarchic systems do not systematically punish dominant firms for mistakes because of their unique position. In fact, the set of conditions that eliminate individual biases is "probably rarely observed in reality" and often does not exist even in financial and commodities markets that mirror most closely the ideal of a fully competitive market (Russell and Thaler 1985, 1071).[1] Indeed, even in competitive markets, evidence suggests that prospect theory explains both individual choices and aggregate market outcomes (Borges 1998). In the study of international relations, realists themselves must acknowledge that the international market for security does not approach a perfectly competitive market. It was the realist emphasis on power that defined the international system in terms of power poles: bipolar, multipolar, and so forth.[2] Such distributions of power do not begin to approach the kind of open competition found in financial or stock markets, where bias still manifests. To the extent that they ally themselves with a particular pole, even relatively weak states are not systematically punished as they rest comfortably under the security umbrella provided by their patron state. Therefore, little support exists for the argument that an imperfect international market for power systematically punishes nonrational choices.[3]

Methodological Arguments

Critics also suggest that the application of prospect theory outside the laboratory raises practical and methodological concerns that, if true, would prove crippling. However, these issues are no more compelling for prospect theory than for rational choice. Therefore, they are best addressed through solid and carefully crafted research.

The first objection is that prospect theory is simply a laboratory artifact resulting from clever wording. In fact, prospect theory's findings are quite robust. Experiments constructed to undermine these findings were unable to do so and instead reconfirmed the basic result (Grether and Plott 1979). Additionally, as noted earlier, considerable evidence suggests that prospect theory explains behavior outside the laboratory, influencing decisions ranging from taxpayer compliance to the selection of medical procedures. The internal logic of prospect theory and its empirical findings are thus quite solid, and there is no reason to reject prospect theory as a contrived artifact simply because it was initially uncovered in a laboratory setting (Levy 1997).

An additional concern is that real-world governments routinely confront knotty foreign-policy problems that are much more complicated than the simple choices given to individuals in the laboratory. In dynamic and fluid decision contexts, scholars will find it difficult to reliably identify the actual reference points adopted by decision makers. Such reference points, even if initially identified, will likely evolve as new information is collected and digested, as relevant actors in the decision ecology change, and as the dynamics of the problem unfold. Without an identifiable reference point against which decision makers can assess prospects as gains or losses, conducting research under prospect theory is impossible. In the laboratory, researchers easily establish and manipulate reference points, and this makes incisive prediction possible. In the real world, no such controls are possible, making the theory difficult to test.

This constitutes a practical objection to the use of prospect theory, not a critique of its empirical findings. A similar critique applies equally to rational choice. It is in fact quite a complicated task to establish empirically that actors both select rational goals and that they are efficient in pursuing them. New information, changing participants, and fluid contexts make it difficult to simultaneously track both the evolving values of policymakers and the criteria by which they evaluate and select alternative strategies.[4]

In response to this complexity, rationalist theory has developed two notions of rationality, procedural and substantive, each with its own empirical domain.[5] Procedural research assumes the content of actor goals and investigates the degree to which individuals maximize them. Substantive research attempts to demonstrate that actors have adopted rational goals given the imperatives that they face, while assuming that actors make maximizing choices in their pursuit. In the study of international politics, dividing the problem this way permits scholars to independently assess the process of goal formation, strategy selection, and choice outcomes. For example, game theory represents the highest form of procedural research. Goals are assumed, and the empirical task is to determine the degree to which states are in fact capable of maximization. By contrast, contemporary realism emphasizes substantive rationality. Rather than attempting to prove that states maximize, realism assumes this and attempts to show that states select substantively rational goals given the imperatives of the international system.

There is an analogy here for prospect theory. Research can focus upon the degree to which state behavior is consistent with prospect theory in a given frame, or it can make the content of the decisional frame itself the focus of study. Given a decisional frame, research would attempt to establish the degree to which states make choices consistent with the predictions of prospect theory, much as empirical game theory attempts to do for procedural rationality. Scholars may also choose to investigate which decisional frame was adopted while assuming prospect theory, rather than rationality, as a model of choice. This parallels the realist project of assuming a decision rule and investigating the degree to which behavior is consistent with a specific set of goals.

Clearly, the most compelling research under rational choice establishes both goals and strategy. Still, the substantive/procedural division is an effective way to deal with the complexity of the social world. It also provides a useful analogy for research deploying prospect theory, suggesting that scholars can deploy it in complex decision environments.

Yet another concern is that the process of real-world decision making does not provide the kind of data required to test a formal model of choice. For example, Boettcher notes that, "Like most formal models of decision making, prospect theory relies on numerically represented probabilities to contribute to the explicitness and accuracy of the model. Yet, when researchers attempt to apply prospect theory to actual cases of foreign policy decision making, they are often forced to rely on verbally represented probabilities. . . . Research in the area of verbal expression of probabilities indicates that these expressions are quite variable" (Boettcher 1995, 563). This is a fundamental objection. It suggests not just that researchers will have difficulty making sense of empirical data when attempting to use prospect theory—as the previous critique suggested—but that necessary data does not exist. It also plagues both rational choice and prospect theory. The requirement for numerical representations of probability stands in "sharp contrast with the fact that people generally prefer to express their beliefs by means of natural language" (Budescu, Weinberg, and Wallsten 1988, 281). Even experts in policy roles often prefer to use general verbal expressions when offering their opinion about alternative strategies.[6]

The lack of precise, verbally represented probabilities is not as compelling a problem as it first appears because it is possible to use the kinds of verbal expressions preferred by policymakers and experts to discriminate between rational choice and prospect theory. For example, McDermott (1998, ch. 2) has shown that specific numerical representations are not required to test hypotheses about framing effects and risk. Instead, we need only evidence about ordinal comparisons. Consider a hypothetical state confronted by two options, A and B, both of which infer gains. Assume that A represents the best outcome if it succeeds and the worst if it fails. Assume also that the best outcome under B is not as good as A, but the costs of failure under B are smaller. We then need only evidence that decision makers view strategy B as more likely to succeed in order to claim that A represents a riskier choice.

In addition, research demonstrates that nonnumerical representations of the disease problem described earlier elicit preference reversals consistent with prospect theory.[7] For example, we can transform the traditional disease problem in the following manner.

Scenario 1

A: Some people will be saved.
B: Some people will be saved or no one will be saved.

Scenario 2

C: Some people will die.
D: Nobody will die or some people will die.

Results show that this reformulation also elicits preference reversal. Individuals favor A in Scenario 1 while preferring B in Scenario 2 (Reyna and Brainerd 1991). Combined, these two examples suggest that scholars can use the verbal formulations preferred by policymakers and experts as data in order to conduct research grounded in prospect theory.

Individual-Based Models and State Choice

A final objection to the use of prospect theory emerges from a long-standing debate in the field about levels of analysis. While prospect theory is a model for individual choice, states are by nature collective entities. The effective decision points within government will vary depending upon, for example, the nature of the issue or the unique institutional arrangements that exist within each state. A theory of state behavior must then also comfortably explain group decisions, control for the influence of institutions, and account for the influence of domestic politics. While prospect theory and rational choice are both individual-level theories, only rational choice has been successful in extending itself to model the dynamics of group and strategic interactions.

One way to address this concern is to redevelop the underlying mathematical logic of prospect theory to account for groups. Fundamental here would be the construction of group-value functions, in which individual functions are transformed to create a single group function. No such research yet exists, and it would be mathematically challenging at best. Fortunately, such an undertaking is unnecessary at this stage in the construction of a cognitive international relations theory.

The consistent finding under prospect theory is that individuals confronted with similar problems make similar choices. So, for example, governments can frame the decision to cooperate in collective action as a set of choices between gains or losses. Once a dominant frame emerges—that is, whenever decision makers share a decision frame—prospect theory predicts that individuals will make similar choices. This does impose limitations on the arguments offered in the following chapters. Evidence from the experimental literature suggests that framing effects break down when individuals confront choice sets that include both gains and losses (Kuhberger 1995). When groups are responsible for foreign policy decisions and individual members operate under competing frame definitions, a prospect theory analysis is inappropriate. Neither is it useful when multiple frames afflict a single decision maker.[8] Notice that the validity of a prospect theory explanation of group decision making turns on the quality of the empirical assertions about the content of shared decision frames. Such explanations cannot be dismissed simply because prospect theory is an individual model of choice.

Importantly, the mechanisms by which group dynamics distort rational decision making are also clear ('t Hart, Stern, and Sundelius 1997). Of particular interest is the dynamic of groupthink, in which a single viewpoint can quickly dominate a group's perspective (Janus 1982). Group leaders can thus define reference points that anchor the group's evaluation of policy options, effectively creating a shared decision frame. Even without this, experimentation suggests that individual cognitive bias surfaces during group decision making (Allision and Messick 1985; Argote, Seabringt, and Dyer 1986). Prospect theory also sways group decisions (Mowen and Gentry 1980; Whyte 1998), and group decision making may amplify framing effects (White 1993). Also interesting here is the finding of a "risky shift" under certain group conditions that is largely consistent with the findings under prospect theory (Moravcsic 1993; Myers and Lamm 1976).[9]

More generally, foreign policy choices fall along a continuum from crisis to routine. The decision point in a crisis is often the national executive. Here, deploying prospect theory is unproblematic. We are applying an individual-based model to an individual. However, under noncrisis conditions additional actors emerge and these, some argue, undermine or dilute the mechanisms of prospect theory. For example, domestic pressure groups often compete for government outputs, and to the extent that any policy hurts some groups and benefits others, the contest of arguments between groups may dilute the influence of prospect theory by creating several competing decision frames as groups lobby policymakers. Here, choice sets include both gains and losses and, as noted above, framing breaks down. However, it is also true that there exists an uneven distribution of both incentives and capacity to form pressure groups. The result is that individual decision anomalies "also reflected in the corresponding interest group, are strengthened at the aggregate level by the intervening bargaining process" (Frey and Eichenberger 1989, 113). Domestic bargaining, therefore, can operate in either direction by ameliorating or exacerbating framing effects, depending upon capacity of lobby groups to define a coherent decision frame. Rather than a theoretical roadblock, the influence of domestic pressure groups is instead an empirical question the answer to which might facilitate or undermine a prospect theory analysis. There also is increasing evidence that prospect theory contours the topography of public opinion concerning national policy initiatives (e.g., Weyland 1996, 1998). Support for a government policy depends crucially upon the frame adopted in the play of competing public discourse. This extends to international policy choices (e.g., Bleckman and Kaplan 1978; Nincic 1997), suggesting that the form and content of communication between national governments and their polities are an important source of framing. Rather than assuming that public opinion nullifies the influence of prospect theory, public opinion is a potentially important and largely unexplored factor in the framing of foreign policy decisions.

These factors are likely to be interactive. The impact of a losses frame held broadly in domestic politics might be undermined as policymakers consider other, possibly more salient international concerns. The opposite may also be true. Aggressive and effective interest-group bargaining could capture policymaker attention and define the status quo for an issue as unacceptable, despite competing definitions from other groups or international partners. Once again, the degree to which theories born from prospect theory are able to explain state behavior is, ultimately, an empirical question.

Finally, independent of these arguments, there is much to recommend grounding social and political theory in an individual model of choice. James Coleman (1990) is a leading modern advocate in this regard, but individualist social theory traces its roots back to the likes of Hobbes, Lock, Rousseau, and Smith. Grounding social theory in individualist assumptions bestows agency, and is thus a necessary condition for understanding the mechanisms by which individual decisions produce social outcomes. An analysis building upon cognitive psychology thus captures the benefits of individualist political theory while simultaneously remaining faithful to the mechanisms of actual human choice.

The use of prospect theory therefore does not however resolve the levels of analysis debate. Locating agency in a unitary actor, small group, or in the play of domestic interest groups and institutions is a theoretical choice. Rationality assumptions are imbedded in theories emphasizing each of these levels. The new models offered here will accept any assumptions about the location of agency commonly used for the body of literature under consideration. This is done both for simplicity's sake, and because it permits a direct comparison of the two perspectives on an equal footing.

Summary

None of the above concerns fatally cripple the enterprise of model building with prospect theory. The empirical findings of prospect theory have proven quite robust, and confirmatory studies outside the laboratory suggest that prospect theory is not simply a contrived artifact of experimentation. Complexity in the social world makes any analysis difficult. However, prospect theory can divide empirical tasks in the same fashion as rational choice. Finally, traditional prospect theory can be used effectively to model the various actors involved in foreign policy decision making. The immediate task for this book therefore remains to construct models of state behavior within a cognitive framework for subsequent empirical examination.

Indeed, and despite the above objections, there already exists considerable research suggesting that prospect theory can generate insights about international politics that run counter to the expectations of rational choice. The section below discusses some of this work to provide a context for the chapters that follow. It is not the purpose of this review to be comprehensive; rather, the discussion below simply establishes that students of international politics have already demonstrated that prospect theory is capable of opening new avenues of inquiry previously closed because the assumption of rational decision making was so dominant. This fact speaks most forcefully for the wider reconsideration of international relations theory that is the purpose of this book.

PROSPECT THEORY AND THE STUDY OF INTERNATIONAL RELATIONS

The Use of Force

Perhaps the most compelling aspect of prospect theory is the finding that as losses emerge, so does risk acceptance.[10] Under conditions of loss, states may risk the use of military force even when the prospects for success are small and even when other options (e.g., diplomacy) contain a higher probability of producing a superior outcome.[11] For example, imagine a state confronted with undesirable changes to the status quo resulting from rival aggression and two available strategies. The first is a military response which provides an opportunity to recover all loss but has a low chance of success, with failure bringing greater loss. The second option is diplomacy. While eliminating loss and returning to the old status quo is unlikely, diplomacy represents the best chance to partially mitigate the consequences of rival action. A choice structured in this way places decision makers in a losses frame. The risk acceptance identified under prospect theory thus predicts that the state will attempt military action, although this option carries with it the largest risks.

British choices during the 1956 Suez Crisis provide evidence for such a dynamic (Richardson 1993). Here, it was the way in which British leaders framed Nasser's action, rather than actual strategic setbacks, that motivated Britain's actions. Confronted with Nasser's nationalization of the Suez Canal, British leaders understood that a military solution was the least likely strategy to return a favorable outcome, but embarked upon an ill-fated military escapade nonetheless. That is, despite considerable evidence that the nationalization of the canal meant little in terms of continued access, Britain's leaders focused "reflexively" upon an "analogy to the disastrous consequences of the appeasement of Hitler" (Richardson 1993, 189). The risks inherent in the military option were known and considerable. They included seriously damaging Britain's position in the region, placing an important ally (the United States) in a very difficult political position, and the near impossibility of success given that, once secured, the canal would require a long and possibly permanent military occupation. Still, Britain opted for the deployment of military force. In the end, this risk acceptant and ultimately ill-fated decision "bears no resemblance to an orthodox expected utility maximization model" and is instead consistent with the predictions of prospect theory (Richardson 1993, 190).

President Carter's 1980 decision to use the military to rescue American hostages held in Iran suggests a similar dynamic (McDermott 1992). As the hostage crisis wore on, a clear losses frame set in for the Carter administration. Growing pressure from Congress, falling domestic popularity, a faltering reelection campaign, and increasing damage to America's international prestige combined to create momentum for action. Still, a rescue mission was not a forgone conclusion. Carter received differing opinions from his advisors, each with their own evaluation of the costs inherent to a continuation of the status quo stalemate. Most importantly, Carter's closest advisor, Secretary of State Cyrus Vance, forcefully argued for caution and against any military action. In Vance's view, "The new status quo, while not optimal, was nonetheless acceptable as long as no one was killed" (McDermott 1992, 248). However, Carter ultimately sided instead with those advisors who viewed current conditions as unacceptable and thought further deterioration was likely.

A rescue mission was viewed by all as a serious escalation with significant costs beyond those of the status quo should the mission fail. The eventual leader of the rescue mission preliminarily assessed the mission as having a "probability of success" of "zero" while entailing considerable risks (McDermott 1992, 257). In fact, all involved maintained beforehand that there was a strong chance that it would fail. The choices facing Carter were similar to the hypothetical lottery presented in chapter 1. The United States faced two prospects. The first was to do nothing militarily and continue with diplomatic pressure. This implied accepting the status quo losses just mentioned. The second was military action. If successful, a rescue mission mitigates all loss, but the likelihood of success was low and failure would surely bring additional losses. Ultimately, in an attempt to return to an acceptable status quo, Carter chose "the riskiest military option seriously considered . . . both in terms of military success as well as in terms of personnel and material costs" because he adopted a losses frame in his definition of the crisis (McDermott 1992, 261).

Prospect theory thus explains why states often too easily resort to force when confronted with losses. It also predicts that states will be slow to deploy force when confronted with gains. To date, research utilizing prospect theory has largely focused upon states making risky choices when facing loss. Far less studied are risk-averse choices under a gains frame.[12] Risk-averse choices are probably less studied for two reasons. First, they are inherently less interesting than risky choices, which have by definition a low probability of success and high costs for failure. Often the result of a risky choice is something other than what the state wanted. Such choices are therefore an attractive focus for study. It is also easier to examine why decision makers made an actual choice than it is to explain why they passed over some particular strategy. Risk aversion often requires that states forgo strategies that might prove profitable, leaving researchers with the difficult task of documenting why a particular outcome never materialized.

Still, while research on risk-averse choice is lacking, imagining the form such explanations would take is not difficult. Consider the policy of appeasement before World War II. In the late 1930s, when assessed against the highly salient horrors of World War I, the postwar peace surely represented a gain over the recent past. When confronted with a resurgent Germany, the allies acted in a predictably risk-averse manner. Operating (if only temporarily) in the domain of gains, the Allies accepted Hitler's promise not to seek another inch of territory in Europe rather than risk a confrontation. Instead of confronting a weaker Germany early, the Allies opted for a conservative strategy in the attempt to avoid losses.[13]

Because states are more likely to risk the use of military force when they face losses than when they must choose between gains, understanding a state's assessment of the status quo is essential to the application of prospect theory. Importantly, Levy has argued that states can identify different reference points for the same status quo and that this might lead them to both perceive a losses frame:

> Consider a situation in which state A has just made tangible gains at state B's expense, say through the seizure of territory or control over a vital operational area. The endowment effect suggests that A will incorporate its gains into an updated status quo much more quickly

> than will B. Consequently, B will attempt to recover its losses and
> restore the old status quo, and A will attempt to maintain the new
> status quo against B's encroachments. Each will accept larger-than-
> normal risks to maintain its version of the status quo. (Levy 1992, 288)

This stylized example highlights the analytic importance of distinguishing between objective and subjective reference points. During the Iran crisis, Carter had several frames of the problem available to him despite the fact that all were looking at the same objective reality. In Levy's example, while one state benefits under current conditions and the other suffers, both are defending their status quo and are therefore more likely to accept the greater risks inherent in a military response. For state A, the status quo and the reference point are the same. Both represent current empirical conditions. For state B, they are distinct. Therefore, we would expect A to adopt a risk-acceptant decision rule only if it viewed B's threats to recoup its own losses as viable. If not, then the status quo is not threatened and A will be risk averse.[14]

This seems to fit Soviet policy prior to the Six Day War (McInerney 1992). Moscow hoped to protect a pro-Soviet regime in Syria, which it viewed as fragile and threatened, by rallying Arab unity within both Syria and the region with artificially inflated estimates of Israeli military capacity and hostile intentions. Soviet leaders did not face actual losses in the Middle East, but rather what they perceived to be a viable future challenge to the status quo in the form of internal and external threats to the new Syrian regime. Deliberately misleading intelligence reports coupled with public declarations from the Soviet government attempted to create the perception that Israel was on the verge of attacking Syria. The risk in this approach is that it would exacerbate existing tensions between Arabs and Israelis and produce the kind of broader conflict that the Soviets most wanted to avoid. Consistent with Levy's hypothetical example, McInerney finds that the Soviets "viewed their new relationship with the Syrians not as a recent gain that could be sacrificed to preserve the peace, but as their reference point from which they did not wish to move" (1992, 277). Moscow was willing to risk a war that would threaten friendly Syrian and Egyptian governments, as well as lead to increased direct U.S. intervention, not because this was desirable but because Soviet leaders adopted a losses frame and subsequently a risk-acceptant strategy. Indeed, in addition to the hoped-for consolidation among Arabs, Soviet actions increased tensions in the region and ultimately produced open conflict with Israel—a conflict Moscow ultimately wanted to avoid.[15]

The finding of loss aversion—related to framing but a distinct finding under prospect theory—suggests that states will pursue more aggressively those strategies intended to avoid loss than strategies that attempt to alter current conditions to accrue new gains. This is the explanation for the finding that loss avoidance produces policies that meet with greater success. For example, U.S. troop deployments to secure political ends have been more successful when the goal was to prevent losses than when the goal was to alter the status quo and secure increased gains (Bleckman and Kaplan 1978). In addition, political leaders get a bigger bump in popularity for protective (loss-avoiding) ventures than they do with promotive (seeking gains over the status quo) foreign policy initiatives (Nincic 1997).

These findings are striking. They demonstrate that there exists broadly in the political landscape a dynamic such that prospect theory contours the domestic political incentive structure that leaders confront.[16] It also supports the above argument that prospect theory—even though it is an individual-level model of decision making—can help us understand the influence of domestic politics on foreign policy choice. This suggests a new angle to the art of political manipulation. Leaders will be more successful in generating domestic political support for foreign action when they couch the justification as loss avoidance, whatever the actual strategic motivation. This kind of framing is possible for any number of important foreign policy concerns: arms control, multilateral peacekeeping efforts, the expansion of NATO, or the promotion of democracy. Taking the latter as an example, leaders could justify increasing a state's international commitments because this improves security by making the world a safer place, or because it avoids loss by holding hostile adversaries at bay. Prospect theory suggests that the second characterization will produce deeper support because it places a discursive emphasis upon loss avoidance.

In summary, the research on prospect theory and international conflict demonstrates that risk acceptance and loss avoidance can lead states to enact risky policies that increase the potential for conflict even when they wish to avoid war. Importantly, the explanation for risky behavior in these studies is not that states misunderstood the implications of their choices, so that what looks to be irrational from an external viewpoint might be rational from the internal perspective of those who participated. Instead, in a direct challenge to rational choice, this research suggests that even when governments carefully consider their options, they nonetheless undertake strategies that are difficult to explain as utility maximizing.

Cooperation

Rational choice predicts that states cooperate only when the benefits of cooperation outweigh the costs, and when it is impossible to secure these same benefits more cheaply through unilateral action. Under prospect theory, evidence suggests that states sometimes frame the decision to cooperate as a risky strategy with a good chance of failure that will result in loss, but one that also carries some smaller chance of success. When operating under a losses frame, governments thus opt for cooperation even when the expected benefits from noncooperation are greater. Now, governments also cooperate in order to minimize expected losses, and this form of loss aversion is wholly consistent with rational choice. Research on prospect theory demonstrates instead that states sometimes choose to cooperate to avoid certain small losses while risking less certain but larger losses.

For example, U.S. decision makers framed the Structural Impediments Initiative with Japan as a "means to avoid short-term tactical and long-term structural losses" (Mastanduno 1993). Faced with a growing trade deficit and an increasingly angry Congress, the Bush administration launched an initiative that would give Japan the right to demand fundamental structural changes in the U.S. economy. This represented a bold and risky strategy whereby the U.S. opened itself to a detailed, comprehensive, and intrusive agreement that impinged upon political and economic policy domains that states usually reserve in defense of their sovereignty.[17] The initiative was a "major gamble" for policymakers, and "created expectations for profound change" (Mastanduno 1993, 38). It was also a significant political risk for an administration often characterized, and increasingly criticized, for its overly conservative foreign policy. In the end, the evidence suggests that risk acceptance and loss avoidance motivated the United States to promote and conclude the agreement, and that it is difficult to explain U.S. behavior as an attempt to maximize other goals like relative or absolute gains.

During the Gulf War, at the request of the United States, Israel declined to respond to Iraqi provocations even as Scud missiles rained down on its metropolitan centers. Such cooperation was risky for Israel.[18] Forbearance threatened to undermine the Israeli security policy, which depended upon the reputation for swift decisive retaliation and military self-reliance. This reputation, Israeli leaders believed, was central to the survival of the state, and undermining it risked a long-cultivated image as a formidable and independent rival. Cooperation thus represented a risk-acceptant strategy designed to mitigate the losses inherent to the status quo (Welch 1993). Despite considerable internal pressure to respond and recent strains in its relationship with the United States, Israel adopted a cooperative strategy while operating in a losses frame.

Prospect theory has also been offered as an explanation for the uneven expansion of multilateral economic surveillance mechanisms built into the International Monetary Fund (Pauly 1993). The puzzle here is to understand why significant resources continue to be dedicated to multilateral surveillance when the usefulness of this mechanism remains in doubt. Specifically, "If the principle behind the function is meaningful, why have states not matched the

Fund's mandate with more substantial authority? If the principle is meaning-less, why have they simply abandoned the function?" (Pauly 1993, 95). One answer is that leaders used the economic chaos of the interwar period as an analogy for the dangers of uncoordinated policy and believed that modifica-tion of the status quo through the establishment of a multilateral monetary surveillance regime might prevent a similar economic collapse. At several junc-tures in the Fund's development, state leaders were in a losses frame. Specifi-cally, whenever the analogy between the interwar economic chaos and worsening existing economic conditions was most manifest in the minds of political leaders, the surveillance provisions of the IMF were strengthened. While multilateral surveillance was viewed as risky and impinging upon sov-ereignty, under a losses frame, leaders pursued that strategy anyway. When leaders did not construct status quo conditions as a loss, they were unwilling to undertake these same risks.

Under a losses frame then, cooperation is sometimes easier to achieve than predicted by rational choice because an expectation of greater benefits to the state is no longer a necessary condition for cooperation. It is also possible for cooperation to be harder to achieve—more difficult, in fact, than is the case under expected utility theory. In addition to the barriers to cooperation iden-tified under traditional theory—among many are dominant incentive games, poor enforcement, imperfect information, and relative gains—prospect theory adds a "concession aversion" (Levy 1996). Recall that the steeper value func-tion for losses means that actors overvalue losses compared to equal gains. In a bargaining context, this means that concessions given will be treated as losses and concessions received treated as gains. If both sides grant equal concessions, loss aversion and the endowment effect predict that both sides will perceive a net loss even if they make equal concessions. Under these conditions, cooper-ation is unlikely as there is a "shrinkage in the size of the bargaining space of mutually beneficial exchanges, a greater tendency to risk the consequences of no agreement or deadlock in an attempt to minimize one's one concessions, and a lower probability of negotiated agreement than utility based bargaining theory might predict" (Levy 1996, 187).

This suggests an alternative explanation for the surveillance mechanisms in the IMF that is also consistent with prospect theory. I discuss it here not because it is a superior explanation, but because it highlights another set of testable propositions consistent with prospect theory. Rather than a risk accep-tant move, one could characterize the establishment of modest surveillance mechanisms as a risk-adverse choice. If the Great Depression was the refer-ence point used by policymakers when considering surveillance mechanisms, then it is possible that leaders were in a gains frame when the actual decisions on surveillance were considered. For each juncture at which changes were under consideration, current conditions would in fact be a considerable improvement over the highly salient Depression era. Under a gains frame, states had two choices. They could enact modest measures to stabilize monetary relations, or they could create new comprehensive and thoroughgoing rules that would promise increased economic gains from deeper cooperation and a more efficient organization of the global economy, but also increase interdependence risks. In a gains frame, prospect theory would predict modest risk-averse measures even if states believed that deeper cooperation would likely bring greater gains. Hence, the modest measures designed to solidify a beneficial status quo may also be consistent with risk aversion.

The fact that interstate cooperation will be more difficult than rational choice predicts in some circumstances, while less difficult in others, adds an additional layer of complexity to the set of hypotheses possible under prospect theory. In expected utility theory, it should not matter how states frame choices attendant to cooperation; they should simply maximize. However, prospect theory suggests that decision-maker evaluations of alternative strategies in terms of gain or loss is an essential component for understanding the selection of a strategy. As demonstrated here, research using prospect theory has focused upon risk acceptance under conditions of loss. While the promise of gain is a necessary condition for cooperation under rational choice, for prospect theory this is not true when states are in a losses frame.

CONCLUSION

Both the framing effect and loss aversion stand in contrast to rational choice and have recently attracted the attention of scholars in international relations. Already, research has found prospect theory useful in understanding why states resort to military force and in identifying a new set of conditions promoting cooperation. Still lacking, however, is an attempt to integrate the various themes in international relations using prospect theory. The above summary of research is not comprehensive, but it does represent fairly the breadth of empirical and theoretical concerns to which prospect theory has been recently applied. Taken collectively, the research thus far does not constitute a viable freestanding alternative to rational choice.

A more comprehensive survey would not change this assessment. Rational choice has spawned an impressive set of interconnected theoretical frameworks including, but not limited to, deterrence, strategic interaction, alliance formation, bargaining, and crisis decision making. It also informs our understanding of war, institutional formation and maintenance, collective action, and economic behavior. To stand as an alternative to rational choice, research on prospect theory must also take up these topics and explore them in a systematic fashion.

This need not imply a single grand theory of politics, but it does require a coherent theoretical treatment of core concepts in the field. One appropriately cautious proponent notes that, while the potential for generating an "interconnected set of propositions about international politics" exists within prospect theory, this potential is yet unrealized (Levy 1997, 107). It will remain unrealized if researchers continue along the path of constructing individualized tests of prospect theory and rational choice. That the research to date has taken this form, rather than first focusing upon theoretical development, is neither surprising nor evidence of some underlying weakness in the approach. The early stages of new research programs often develop similarly, as scholars try out new ideas and learn to operationalize concepts.

I would argue that this initial stage is complete, that prospect theory has made an initial contribution to the international relations literature by promoting a new set of important questions and offering some answers. Such an opening is quintessentially scientific, forcing established theory to confront new and difficult empirical concerns. What is needed now that prospect theory has demonstrated a capacity to explain state behavior is the construction of a larger set of interconnected propositions about international politics like that which already exists for rational choice.

Chapter 3

The Use of Power

INTRODUCTION

Prospect theory stands as a coherent alternative to rationality as a cornerstone for the construction of international relations theory. While methodological concerns exist, none are so compelling as to represent a roadblock to the further development of prospect theory into a framework for international political analysis. This chapter first elaborates upon the concept of a decision frame. Next, decision frames are used to reassess the role of power and coercion in international politics. Particular emphasis is given to the unintended consequences of military and economic threats that are hidden by rational choice, but that reveal themselves under prospect theory.

STATUS QUO, SUBJECTIVITY, AND DECISION FRAMES

Under prospect theory, decision makers are risk averse when confronted with a choice between a sure gain and a lottery, while risk acceptant when confronted with a choice between certain loss and a lottery. These two findings can be applied to any substantive issue, for example, deterrence, cooperation, and environmental protection. Indeed, the previous chapter demonstrated that they have already been examined in some depth. However, states often face choices not between two narrowly defined alternatives to the status quo, but rather between the status quo and change. For example, a state might have to choose between absorbing the costs of recent rival incursions and a risky military response, or between recent economic growth and risky cooperation offering further potential benefits. Initially, such choice sets do not seem to fit under an analysis using prospect theory because actors are not choosing between two clearly defined alternatives to the status quo.

The issue here is reference points. Initial experiments presented choice sets to subjects such that an individual's status quo endowment represented the reference point. Thus, as in the original formulation of prospect theory, individuals were confronted with two alternatives to the status quo. Subsequent investigation revealed that a variety of factors can influence the construction of reference points. Consider the following example. A gambler at the local race track has, throughout the course of a day's betting, lost $140. Now, on the final race of the day, he is contemplating a $10 bet on a 15:1 long shot. Two different frames are possible: "If the status quo is the reference point, the outcomes of the bet are framed as a gain of $140 and a loss of $10. On the other hand, it may be more natural to view the present state as a loss of $140, for the betting day, and accordingly frame the last bet as a chance to return to the reference point or to increase the loss to $150" (Tuersky and Kahneman 1981, 456). Decision makers can thus retain their old reference points for a time by using the recent past as a cognitive anchor against which they evaluate recent changes.[1] In this example, two different decision frames are possible for a single set of objective conditions. In the second construction—a losses frame—the status quo and reference points are distinct, such that the recent changes replace the "sure thing" in the standard choice set for prospect theory. Figure 3.1 graphically depicts the relationship between the status quo and recent change. Recent beneficial changes to the status quo sit outside the reference point at the graph's origin. The choice is between accepting the benefits from recent changes and attempting to secure still further gain in the form of a lottery.

Depending upon the nature of the change, a gains or losses frame will exist for some period after change has occurred. The speed with which updating takes place, or "how long one retains an original point of reference," is an important question for prospect theorists (Shafir 1992, 316). Jervis suggests that "[i]n international politics—and in social life in general . . . we renormalize for gains much more quickly than we do for losses. We rapidly, if not effortlessly, adjust to good fortune and any improvement in our lives. . . . Neither individuals nor nations are so accepting of losses, however. We remain unhappy, unreconciled, and often bitter for a prolonged period" (Jervis 1992, 200). This observation is supported by the asymmetrical s-shaped value function, which captures the fact that losses loom subjectively larger than equal gains. Additionally, the endowment effect discussed in chapter 1 demonstrates that individuals consistently offer to pay less money to purchase an item than they would be willing to sell it for once it is possessed. Actors consistently

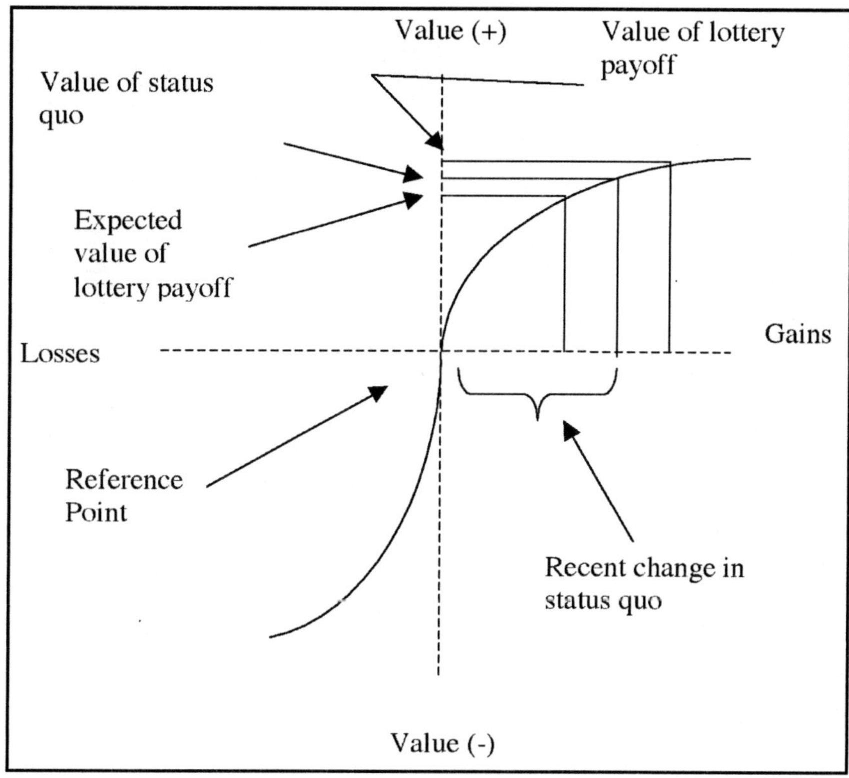

FIGURE 3.1. The decision frame for recent positive changes in the status quo. Recent changes represent the "sure thing" in the standard prospect theory choice set, and represent an outcome distinct from the reference point.

overvalue that which they already own, and so renormalize for gains more quickly than for losses (Levy 1992, 290). This tendency for losses to linger is, though, at best a rough guide to research rather than an ironclad theory of updating. Ultimately, decision maker assessments about the value of the status quo are an empirical question. Such judgments cannot be prespecified theoretically. Neither can we predetermine precisely how far into the future decision makers look in their valuation of the status quo. Shifts in the decision frame reflect objective changes, but the two may not coincide entirely.

In fact, a number of subjective factors can affect the content of a decision frame. These include "social norms and expectations," one's "level of aspiration," or simply the "state to which one has adapted" (Tversky and Kahneman

1981, 456). One could instead simply assume a close correlation between a state's objective circumstances and decision maker perceptions. This would require an assumption that actors accurately perceive recent changes in the status quo and, therefore, that objective measures provide a guide to the content of the decision frame. However, decision makers often operate under consistent world views that persist even as surrounding conditions change. Political subjectivity can therefore play an important role in the construction of decision frames. The possibility of a socially constructed frame—that is, where only perception is operative regardless of objective circumstances— exists and is consistent with Kahneman and Tversky's observation that there are many cases in which "the reference point is determined by events that are only imagined" (1982, 171–72). The assertion of a frame that stands against objective conditions is therefore a theoretical possibility, but it would require thorough documentation.

It is therefore possible under prospect theory to examine decisions where governments must choose between clearly defined alternatives to the status quo, and where they must choose between the status quo and change.[2] Building on this insight, the following sections undertake an analysis of the application of state power.[3] Under the framework offered here, a state's risk disposition, rather than the credibility of rival threats or the cost of imposed sanctions, emerges as the central variable explaining the policy decisions of governments.

POWER AND COERCION

Prospect theory opens new insights into the dynamics of power politics. Most importantly, the content of decision frames can be unintentionally altered or deliberately manipulated through the application of state power. If decision makers possessed an explicit understanding of prospect theory, then manipulation of frames would be deliberate. Lacking such knowledge, most instances of manipulation are likely unintentional. Altering the content of the decision frame is therefore an important unexplored consequence of power politics, the implications of which are central to an understanding of state behavior. Often, research on coercion suggests that states confronted by rival power alter their preferences by scaling back their goals; that is, governments simply alter their expectations about the potential benefits of a particular strategy (for example, less territory, smaller economic gains, and so forth). Prospect theory adds to this the observation that states may also radically—but predictably—alter their strategies. Consequently, rational choice and prospect theory differ sharply over what constitutes an effective application of power.

Typically, an attempt to alter or deter unwanted rival state behavior involves two steps: threats followed by sanction. The initial deployment of threats serves several practical purposes. Threats initially tie explicit negative consequences to unwanted behavior. Threats also hold the possibility of achieving one's goals without actually having to pay the costs associated with punishing a transgression. The idea is to communicate compelling and credible threats, so that the target understands clearly that painful consequences will follow undesirable behavior. If threats fail, sanctions usually follow, making real the negative consequences of unwanted behavior.

While threats and sanctions represent distinct policies, from the perspective of prospect theory they share an important consequence. Each holds the potential to pitch the target into a losses frame and thereby induce unwanted risk-acceptant behavior. Under a losses frame, the target of threats or sanctions might act quite contrary to the wishes of the threatening state, and contrary to the predictions of rational choice. Thus, prospect theory adds to our understanding of military and economic coercion an understanding of how certain types of threatening or sanctioning may inadvertently produce the very behavior that such policies are designed to prevent.

MILITARY DETERRENCE

As both an academic theory and a strategic policy, military deterrence relies fundamentally upon the assumption of rational states. The logic of deterrence is commonly depicted as a game of chicken.[4] The standard assumption built into such models is that governments each prefer mutual cooperation under the status quo to war, but that each would also prefer an advantage over their rival to the status quo. As in shown in figure 3.2, states have two choices. They can cooperate through restraint, or attempt to revise the status quo and impose a new settlement. If both states exercise restraint, deterrence succeeds and the status quo continues. If either aggresses, deterrence has failed. Mutual aggression represents the least desirable outcome.

One compelling aspect of this relationship is that the credibility of deterrence threats is undermined by the structure of the game. Each state has an incentive to be the first to move off the status quo because, once such a move is made, continued cooperation is the maximizing strategy for the target of aggression (Zagare 1990). Assuming both states understand this, we should observe in chicken games an immediate race to defection.

Nevertheless, deterrence is often successful. Proponents of rational deterrence argue that such success is the result of the capacity of states to offer contingent commitment threats. Successful threats are those that are credible,

<table>
<tr><td rowspan="2"></td><td colspan="2" align="center">State A</td></tr>
<tr><td align="center">Cooperate</td><td align="center">Defect</td></tr>
<tr><td>Cooperate</td><td align="center">3, 3</td><td align="center">2, 4</td></tr>
<tr><td>Defect</td><td align="center">4, 2</td><td align="center">1, 1</td></tr>
</table>

State B

FIGURE 3.2. A standard deterrence game

forcing potential aggressors to settle for the status quo. While this appears to resolve the deterrence paradox, it raises an equally difficult question. How do contingent commitments deter when it is irrational for a state to carry out retaliation once deterrence has failed? One unsatisfactory answer is that rational decision makers will meaningfully commit to a deterrence strategy if, in the long run, the commitment brings a higher expected payoff than no commitment. For example, "[I]t is rational to execute the intention [to retaliate] if and only if it is utility maximizing to form it. From this follows that since it may be rational to form the intention to execute the threat, it may also be rational to carry it out. . . . if the intention has been formed, and deterrence fails, then a rational agent who intends to retaliate should do so because acting upon this intention is part of the behavior required of an expected utility maximizer" (Zagare 1990, 252). The contention here is that deterrence breaks down when governments fail to construct a preference for carrying out a contingent commitment, or when a state fails to recognize that their rival actually formed such a preference. The success of a deterrent, then, lies in communicating the fact that one has formed a preference for action that is irrational at the time it must be taken, but rational at the time the commitment is made.

Prospect theory identifies a different set of conditions that predict when deterrence will succeed or fail. Deterrence threats are more likely to be effective when both states are in a gains frame than when one or both states are operating under a losses frame. Under a gains frame, governments will not risk disturbing a beneficial status quo even if the expected benefits of defection are greater than continued cooperation, so long as defection also contains some smaller chance of no gain. This means that less than perfectly credible threats will provide a meaningful deterrent. In a losses frame, decision makers are risk acceptant and thus more willing to risk the prospect of open conflict if they also perceive some chance of limiting existing losses. Here, credible deterrent threats may not provide a sufficient deterrent.

Typically, incentives for a deterrence game—like those given in figure 3.2—are depicted as rank-ordered preferences. While ranking provides information about the relative value of outcomes, it tells us nothing about which outcomes are acceptable to decision makers. To the extent that assessments about acceptability determine which outcomes decision makers place placed in a gains or losses frame, such evaluations are essential to an analysis using prospect theory. Including an indication of acceptability also helps clarify problematic assumptions in traditional theory about state motivations. The fact that there are potential gains to be secured by upsetting the status quo does not mean, as the theory of deterrence often seems to imply, that each state is dissatisfied with a stalemate. Under the traditional depiction of incentives, even those states that find themselves largely satisfied with the status quo will be tempted by defection. That is, in order to improve their position, traditional theory implies that states will risk war by attempting to overturn an acceptable status quo.[5]

Figure 3.3 displays a set of outcomes that is consistent with a standard deterrence game, although it presents payoffs in intervals. Positive values represent levels of satisfaction over an acceptable status quo, and negative values depict increasing dissatisfaction. The preference order here is identical to the traditional game. That is, the use of intervals does not alter the incentive structure. Interval payoffs simply include a representation about the acceptability of outcomes in relation to decision maker reference points. Each state can still gain by unilateral defection. However, we can now determine whether or not status quo represents a satisfactory outcome. Mutual cooperation is still preferred to unilateral cooperation, and this is still preferred to war. Deterrent threats in this game must still overcome the fact that once a rival defects, the best strategy is to capitulate. By the traditional view, then, the games are identical so that a threat that is effective for the traditional game in figure 3.2 would also deter rivals in figure 3.3.

Assuming interval payoffs, under prospect theory, the two games are quite different. In figure 3.3, the status quo of cooperation is unacceptable, and both states must therefore choose between accepting existing losses or risking a costly war as part of a move toward an acceptable condition. As noted earlier, traditional deterrence theory emphasizes the importance of rival deterrent threats. At best such threats are largely, but imperfectly, credible. States must

	State A	
	Cooperate	Defect
State B Cooperate	-3, -3	-5, -1
Defect	-1, -5	-9, -9

FIGURE 3.3. A chicken game with states under a losses frame

therefore choose between accepting the certain smaller losses inherent to the status quo, or pursuing a gamble that contains greater expected losses, but that also contains some small prospect of minimizing losses. Such states are confronted with a losses frame, and prospect theory predicts that they will opt for the gamble. Risk acceptance in the face of losses has historical precedent. For example, in their critique of rational deterrence, Lebow and Stein note that Egypt's 1973 decision to overrun the status quo was not the result of failed Israeli deterrence threats. Instead, it was related to Egyptian status quo evaluations and resultant risk acceptance:

> If Egyptian leaders had miscalculated, proponents of deterrence might argue that human error accounted for its failure. . . . [However], Egypt's leaders decided to challenge deterrence not because they erred, but because they considered the domestic and foreign costs of inaction unbearably high. They correctly anticipated a major military response by Israel, and they expected to suffer significant casualties and losses. Nevertheless, they planned a limited military action to disrupt the status quo. . . . Egyptian leaders considered their military capabilities inferior to those of Israel, but chose to use force because they anticipated grave domestic and strategic consequences from continuing inaction. (Lebow 1987, 12)[6]

Now reconsider figure 3.2 using interval payoffs. This represents deterrence for states in a gains frame. Here, leaders face a different set of alternatives: accept the certain gains of continued cooperation, or attempt to improve their position while risking war. Even if we assume that governments in this game attach only moderate levels of credibility to their rival's deterrence threats, risk aversion leads states to opt for the certain gains of the status quo. Deterrence is thereby maintained even if the expected gains from aggression are greater than those from cooperation.

Deterrence relationships are therefore much more stable when both states are in a gains frame. The success of deterrence no longer depends exclusively upon the credibility of deterrent threats. Just as important are each participant's assessments about the acceptability of the status quo.

Prospect theory thus explains why deterrence sometimes fails despite the fact that states routinely adopt the strategies recommended by rational deterrence theory. Two distinct but related dynamics are at work here. First, under rational choice, the difference between perfect and near-perfect credibility is unimportant. Proponents of traditional theory would therefore object to the characterization that states in a losses frame, when confronted with credible deterrence threats, face a choice between a sure loss and a gamble. Instead, credible deterrence threats impose upon rivals a choice between two (near) certain outcomes: the status quo and a loss. While no deterrent threat is perfectly credible, the discount in expected value between the certain and near certain is often so small that in such cases a strategy of aggression is not a gamble in any meaningful sense of the term. Instead, it produces an expected value that is practically indistinguishable from the certain value of open conflict. Even if the findings of prospect theory were valid, such an analysis in this case is inappropriate because, to the extent that states can craft credible deterrents, the choice set confronting rival governments is different in structure from that which elicits framing effects.

However, prospect theory has demonstrated that individuals consistently deviate from rational choice in making assessments about probabilities at the extremes of the distribution. Laboratory experimentation confirms that decision makers overweight low probability events and underweight high probability events (see Kahneman and Tversky, 1982). The subjective difference between a certain outcome and one with a probability of, say, 92 percent, is larger than the difference between two outcomes with the same difference somewhere in the middle of the probability distribution (for example, 58 percent versus 50 percent). For a government operating under a losses frame, the difference in value between certain and near certain deterrence threats is therefore subjectively greater than traditional theory has heretofore assumed. This means that decisions makers do not, as traditional theory implies, view the choice set as constituting two certain outcomes involving loss. Rather, the context produces a classic prospect theory choice between a sure thing and a gamble. Risk acceptance, even in the face of highly credible deterrent threats, can lead to defection.

Traditionalists would nonetheless argue that the appropriate response would be to overbuild deterrence capacity and leave no doubt about one's ability to execute deterrence threats; the larger the deterrent capacity, the more credible the deterrent. Ideally, the goal should be to construct a deterrent capacity compelling enough to overwhelm the possibility of rival misperception which might lead to aggression (Steinbruner 1976). If one source of misperception comes from mistakes regarding probability assessments, the traditional view would still provide an effective set of strategic recommendations that would produce successful deterrence.

However, perhaps the most pernicious characteristic of anarchic systems is that defensive preparations can create a security dilemma for rivals, making them feel less secure. Indeed, creating insecurity is the goal of states locked in traditional deterrence games. The idea is to undermine rival confidence that aggression will produce an advantage. Insecurity should then generate conservative, risk-averse strategies.

Under prospect theory, producing insecurity also has consequences for rival assessments about status quo that are quite apart from those that would result from actually implementing a threat. Where insecurity is extreme, security dilemmas are akin to a losses frame. For example, the implications for the deployment of space-based weapons can be twofold. Traditional theory argues that deployment communicates an increased capacity to punish rivals for their transgressions. However, it also produces a permanent relative military disadvantage for the target of deterrence, a losses frame for the status quo, and thereby an increased chance of risk-acceptant aggression. Rather than continually increasing deterrent capacities with no logical upper limit, as prescribed by traditional doctrine, prospect theory demonstrates instead that moderate deterrents will be more successful because they are less likely to generate a losses frame and risk-acceptant decisions.

The relationships defined by figure 3.4 capture this point. Here, the incentive structure facing both states is consistent with the original formulation of deterrence. State A is in a losses frame, in part, because of the new rival military deployments that force a reevaluation of the status quo. Meanwhile, state B remains in a gains frame due to these same preparations. The analysis above explains why B will continue to be deterred by less than fully credible threats by A. However, A will seek to revise the status quo even if confronted by highly credible deterrence threats from B. The development of increasingly potent deterrents is rational for B under traditional theory. However, it does not produce the desired result to the extent that this strategy is responsible for A's reevaluation of the status quo.

<table>
<tr><td rowspan="2"></td><td rowspan="2"></td><td colspan="2" align="center">State A</td></tr>
<tr><td align="center">Cooperate</td><td align="center">Defect</td></tr>
<tr><td rowspan="2">State B</td><td>Cooperate</td><td align="center">4, -2</td><td align="center">2, -1</td></tr>
<tr><td>Defect</td><td align="center">5, -3</td><td align="center">1, -4</td></tr>
</table>

FIGURE 3.4. Asymetric chicken game
State A operates under a losses frame, state B under a gains frame.

Importantly, the mechanism behind A's aggression is distinct from the traditional notion of a preemptive strike. Preemption is a rational strategy intended to deny rivals future advantage. Once a rival has secured an advantage, the incentive to preempt dissipates because the new capacity is part of the rival deterrent. Thus, developing new capacity is destabilizing until fully deployed; after that, new capacities become part of a more effective deterrent and stability returns to the relationship. Prospect theory demonstrates that the destabilizing effect of deployments can persist after they are fully implemented. To the extent that new capacity constitutes a greater security threat and contributes to a losses frame, deployment may produce long-run risk acceptance and is therefore potentially destabilizing. There is, then, an important distinction to be made between the logic of preemption as described by traditional theory and the risk acceptant aggression predicted by prospect theory.

The set of structures defining the universe of actual deterrence incentives obviously extends beyond the chicken game. However, even with this limited analysis, prospect theory identifies a new set of conditions for successful deterrence. Under traditional theory, the goal of deterrence is to construct credible deterrents. While this remains a sound strategy under prospect theory, it must avoid—to the extent possible—contributing to a rival losses frame and inducing risk-acceptant behavior. Prospect theory demonstrates that deterrence will be more effective when the target of deterrence is not in a losses frame, and thus also forces a distinction between credible threats and effective military deterrence. Traditional theory emphasizes credibility, but this is not a sufficient condition for successful deterrence. To the extent that deterrence threats deliberately or inadvertently force rivals to reevaluate the desirability of the status quo, such threats may contribute to the behavior they are intended to deter. Clearly, as explained earlier, any number of objective or subjective factors can contribute to a losses frame. Prospect theory cautions nonetheless that deterrents should be sufficient to inflict losses on rivals, but avoid pitching them into a losses frame.[7]

ECONOMIC THREATS

Despite the deepening of multilateral institutions over the last two decades, in an anarchic international system, threats remain the common currency of international politics, and the proper deployment of threats lies at the core of effective statecraft. States issue economic threats to promote political agendas and to protect their commercial interests. Despite trends suggesting that economic threats are increasingly common, there is little consensus on the effectiveness of such threats, and their utility as a policy instrument remains very much in doubt (Haass 1997; Lindsday 1986).

Prospect theory and rational choice sharply differ over the factors that define successful threatening. Traditional theory tells us that threats must be credible and that the potential cost of absorbing a threat's implementation must outweigh the net benefits that the target derives from the status quo. Prospect theory demonstrates that assessments concerning the acceptability of the status quo are equally important and cautions that some of the strategies suggested by rational choice will ultimately prove counterproductive to the state initiating the threat.

TWO-LEVEL ECONOMIC THREAT MODEL

In military affairs, the assumption that states are unified actors is often both theoretically useful and empirically justified because security threats place all domestic actors at equal risk. By contrast, economic threats usually harm some constituents while leaving others unscathed.[8] Combined with the fact that domestic constituents are not political equals, this suggests that the assumption of unified actors common in deterrence theory misses important aspects of economic threatening. As a model of decision making, prospect theory can be integrated into existing theory concerning the role of domestic politics. As with deterrence theory, prospect theory produces insights that both confront and confirm our conventional understanding.

Putnam's (1988) two-level game framework explicitly rejects unified state assumptions and is therefore well positioned to examine the uneven effect of economic threats upon varied domestic groups. The basic idea is that political leaders are constrained by the interests of domestic actors and that these constraints create a win-set, defined as the range of acceptable outcomes to empowered domestic constituents. The understanding of international relations that flows from this view is that "[t]he politics of many international negotiations can usefully be conceived as a two-level game. At the national level, domestic groups pursue their interests by pressuring the government to adopt favorable policies, and politicians seek power by constructing coalitions among those groups. At the international level, national governments seek to maximize their own ability to satisfy domestic pressures, while minimizing the adverse consequences of foreign developments" (Putnam 1988, 434). In two-level terms, the political objective behind economic threats is to expand the target state's win-set by mobilizing domestic actors in support of the threatening state's position. The key here is that "those constituents whose interests are most affected [in the target state] will exert special influence" over the target policies, and therefore over the range of outcomes that would constitute an acceptable compromise (Putnam 1988, 446). For the government initiating a threat, the prospects for a favorable settlement increase as the rival domestic win-set expands.

The previous section demonstrated that one possible consequence of credible and highly punitive threats is that the cost of their implementation becomes the reference point against which decision makers in the target evaluate available strategies. Under two-level logic, this dynamic is more likely when economic threats target heretofore neutral groups that have no stake in the current dispute, and less likely when threats target groups with a vested interest in the status quo. Threats against neutrals are more likely to create a losses frame, and therefore hold greater potential to induce risk-acceptant behavior that can take the form of firm intransigence—even in the face of threats that rational analysis would find compelling. Rational choice, by contrast, argues that it is precisely such threats against neutrals that are most effective. Neutrals are easier to motivate than vested interests because threats against them can be smaller and therefore more credible.

Imagine two states, A and B, in a trade dispute. Assume that A initiates threats to recover losses that are the direct result of B's mercantilist policies. Within A, there is a damaged domestic constituent that suffers as a result of B's action. Within B, there is a constituency that benefits from the same policy. In both A and B, there are neutral constituents that remain initially unaffected by their governments' dispute. Figure 3.5 adapts a standard two-level game to represent the continuum of possible outcomes in this dispute. The far right represents B's preference for retaining the gains enjoyed under the status quo; the far left represents A's desire to have B remove discriminatory barriers.

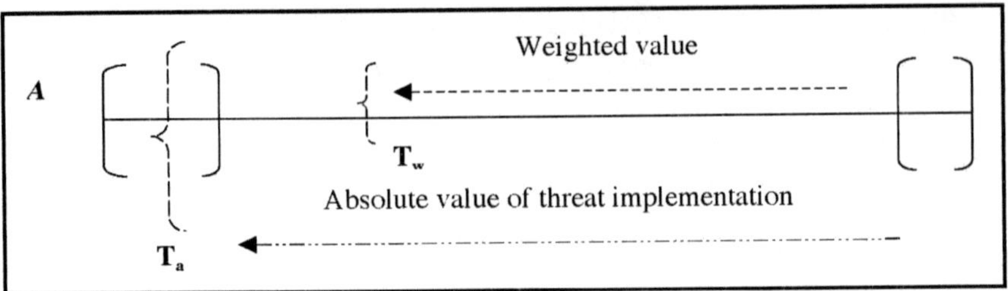

FIGURE 3.5. Economic threats in a two-level game
Solid brackets represent each state's initial winset. T_w depicts the discount
on the absolute value of threat T_a, due to imperfect credibility.

Initially, win-sets are defined by the groups in each state that are affected by
B's protection of its domestic markets. The bracketed space represents this for
each state.

As explained above, a successful threat is defined as one that can impose
external costs sufficient to broaden the win-set of the target. A's threats are
successful to the extent that they can pull the interior bracket of B's win-set
outward to overlap with its own. The magnitude of shifts is a direct function
of the absolute value of the threat weighted by its credibility. For example, if
A's threat is perfectly credible, we can expect a widening of the target's win-set
exactly equal to the value of the threat. However, the credibility of threats is
significantly determined by degree to which powerful domestic groups support
such a policy (Moravcsic 1993, 29). An important determinant of domestic
support is the degree to which groups at home will have to endure the costs
that result from the threat's implementation. That is, implementation imposes
costs on the initiating state as well as the target. Economic threats are therefore always less than completely credible. Embargos hurt domestic producers
through reduced demand; tariffs harm domestic manufacturers who utilize the
targeted imports in the manufacture of finished products. Were it otherwise—
that threats could be implemented cost free—credibility would not be an issue
and attempts at coercion would be much more common. As the domestic costs
of implementation rise, the credibility of threats declines.

Rational Choice, Economic Threats, and Domestic Politics

There are then two strategies available to aggrieved states like A. They can
either target constituents that have an interest in the status quo, or they can
target heretofore neutral constituents. Groups benefiting from protection will

resist giving up the rents enjoyed under existing policies and will initially oppose attempts to alter the status quo through negotiation. Figure 3.5 demonstrates why the discount of imperfect credibility requires that the absolute value of a successful threat against these benefiting groups must be greater than the value of protection enjoyed under the status quo. Threats of lesser (or equal) value will not compel these interests to lobby their government for a settlement favorable to damaged groups in the threatening state.

A second strategy is to target neutrals. The intent here is to overcome domestic opposition to a settlement by activating heretofore uninterested political actors and marshaling new social forces in favor of a resolution. Initially, neutral constituents are by definition agnostic with respect to changes in the status quo and, therefore, from the point of view of their government, politically irrelevant. Unlike benefiting constituents, neutrals have no initial stake in their government's intransigence. As a result, any threat targeted at neutrals represents a potential loss when compared to the status quo. Targeted neutral groups will then favor settlement, whatever the level of proposed sanction against them. The imposed cost of sanctions required to convert neutrals to the threatening state's policies is therefore considerably less than that which would be required to convince currently benefiting groups to support a favorable settlement.

According to rational choice, the most efficient and effective strategy for A is to level threats against neutral constituencies in B. Successful threatening of neutrals requires targeting groups that possess greater political weight than those groups currently benefiting under the status quo. If there are no neutral interests of such influence and importance—or if threats against them are not possible—the strategy suggests threatening many smaller groups. Either approach can construct a countercoalition in B's domestic polity to widen the win-set. Otherwise, the attempt to alter the preference of benefiting constituents must overcome the gains from intransigence, and this requires larger threats with a concurrent increase in the domestic costs of implementation and, therefore, a decrease in credibility. The domestic cost of implementation against neutrals is comparatively lower, and the credibility of such threats is thereby increased.

Prospect Theory, Economic Threats, and Domestic Politics

Prospect theory predicts that threats against neutrals may be inadvertently counterproductive because of their impact upon the target's assessments of the status quo. Recall from chapter 2 that credible challenges to the status quo often become the reference point against which decision makers evaluate alternative strategies and outcomes. Credible challenges produce a losses frame wherein a government will "accept larger-than-normal risks in order to maintain its version of the status quo" (Levy 1992, 288).

Essentially, the dilemma is that by targeting more powerful neutrals threatening states place their counterparts in a losses frame because credible threats against neutrals are more likely to represent a viable challenge to the status quo than less credible threats against vested groups. Such threats force a choice between accepting the political and economic losses that come from appeasement and gambling that rivals will not execute sanctions that carry still greater political costs. Intransigence risks these larger losses. Whenever there is also even a small chance that the threatening state will back down, prospect theory predicts that states will gamble in an attempt to return to an acceptable status quo. That is, even if threats are credible—indeed because they are credible—loss aversion and risk acceptance prevail. Of course, risky behavior could include any number of strategies beyond intransigence. Aggressive counter threatening might result. The point here is that where rational choice predicts that threats against neutrals would be the best strategy, prospect theory predicts that this same strategy might produce unintended consequences in the form of risky rival behavior.

A similar dynamic applies if the initiating government levels threats more broadly by targeting a number of less influential neutral groups. As noted in chapter 2, previous research has established that prospect theory takes hold in domestic politics such that leaders gain more support when they undertake actions that are justified to the public as loss avoiding rather than gains seeking. Standing up to a powerful rival may sometimes seem like a hopeless endeavor from the perspective of rational choice. This is especially true when rivals attempt to create broad public support in favor of their preferred outcome. However, this intransigence is precisely what prospect theory predicts will happen when states target large numbers of domestic interests.

Prospect theory is thus more pessimistic about the utility of economic threatening than is rational choice. Under rational choice, the failure of threats to produce desired results stems from their inappropriate application. The threatening government failed to select the appropriate target or did not communicate its intentions with sufficient clarity and credibility. By contrast, prospect theory suggests that even when all the sufficient conditions (as per rational choice) are met, states may still find frustration in the form of an obstinate rival willing to undertake seemingly inordinate risks in an attempt to return to an acceptable position. This result may explain why, as noted above, the utility of threats is undergoing reexamination. The mounting evidence that they are often ineffective is in part attributable to the framework outlined here.

This also suggests a new set of research priorities. Less important are those factors that influence the credibility of a threat; a traditional emphasis in the literature. As in the previous section, threats will be more effective—whatever their credibility—when the target is not in a losses frame. Research should explore first the empirical relationship between the onset of a losses frame and the success or failure of economic threats. In addition, greater attention should be placed upon those factors that contribute to a losses frame with emphasis upon the extent to which threats are themselves responsible.

THE FAILURE OF SANCTIONS

A similar mechanism operates when threats fail and states impose sanctions. Despite their increasing popularity as a "liberal alternative to war," the empirical record on the ability of sanctions to produce desired outcomes places the utility of this strategy very much in doubt (Pape 1997, 90).[9] Virtually all of the literature on economic sanctions in both economics and international relations has modeled states as unitary rational actors (Kaempfer and Lowenberg 1999). Yet sanctioning policies largely guided by this assumption have failed to produce the predicted results. There are two widely held explanations for this failure. Failed sanctions are either poorly targeted or they inadvertently create a "rally around the flag" effect that benefits incumbent governments. The first explanation is that sanctioning states fail to deny the target some important commodity. It is difficult to assure universal cooperation in a sanctioning effort. Often, third parties seek their own gain by providing goods and services to the target, thus undermining the intended impact of sanctions. Where this dynamic exists, the reason for the failure of sanctions needs no further explanation. Such sanctions are simply too weak to expect that they will motivate the desired changes in rival policy.[10]

However, the second explanation for the failure of sanctions is more problematic. Here sanctions do impose significant economic and social pain, but the target government nonetheless refuses to capitulate. Often, this is true even when the target is considerably weaker than the sanctioning state. Economic hardship that is clearly the result of powerful external rivals unintentionally generates support for the existing government and its policies. One study notes that "none of this is surprising. The spectacle of an implacably hostile superpower wielding its economic might against a weak and beleaguered nations will usually rouse the patriotic indignation of its populations and generate a rally around the flag effect to the government's benefit" (Nincic and Wallensteen 1983, 6).

Obstinacy in the face of sanctions that are greater than the costs of policy modification is clearly nonmaximizing. However, an explanation for this phenomenon does not require that we invent a whole new set of political and social dynamics to explain it. A more elegant solution is possible under prospect theory. It is simply that economic sanctions contribute to a losses frame, and this produces risk-acceptant strategies. Domestic support for government intransigence in the face of biting sanctions is the result of societal decisions—filtered through prospect theory—about the domestic costs and benefits of intransigence.

We know from previous research that governments have capitalized upon a losses frame to gain support for risky and thoroughgoing changes in domestic policy, even when citizens understand that such changes would likely bring further loss (Weyland 1996). This same dynamic applies to foreign policy decisions. For the duration of sanctions, governments face two options, each of which implies losses. They can capitulate, altering their policy so that it is consistent with the sanctioning state's demands. This would bring the known certain losses that result from policy modification. Alternatively, the sanctioned government can risk intransigence. Even if we assume the difficult case in which the cost of sanctions is greater than the costs of policy adjustment, prospect theory predicts that the target will risk intransigence if it believes that this strategy also contains some chance of minimizing losses—that is, so long as it is believed that there is some chance that sanctioners will tire of the effort or scale back their demands. Intransigence thus represents a risk-acceptant strategy aimed at mitigating the status quo losses resulting from sanctions.

As with threatening, prospect theory is more pessimistic than rational choice regarding the usefulness of sanctions. However, this pessimism does not imply that any attempt to tie punishment to unwanted action will inevitably fail. Instead, the implication of prospect theory is that threats or sanctions are effective when the target of such attempts is in a gains frame and risk averse. For example, states are less likely to risk sanctions if they find the status quo acceptable. This suggests that a strategy tying positive incentives and sanctions together will be the most effective approach. A sanctions package that includes rewards for good behavior, if it does not create a gains frame, at the very least inoculates against the onset of a losses frame to the extent that the target must consider both gains and losses simultaneously. As noted earlier, when both gains and losses exist within a choice set framing effects tend to break down. This makes risk-acceptant, nonmaximizing intransigence less likely.

CONCLUSION

In addition to circumstances wherein states confront two well defined alternatives to the status quo, it is also possible to deploy prospect theory in cases where states face a choice between the status quo and change. Whether the decision frame is structurally determined, socially constituted, or both remains an empirical question that must be established in each instance. Note, however, that the original formulation of prospect theory permits that "the reference point is determined by events that are only imagined," suggesting that wholly constituted frames are possible (Kahneman and Tversky 1982, 171–72). Decision frames may bear little resemblance to the real world but prove to be politically compelling nonetheless.

The notion of a decision frame also begs the question of manipulation. Frames can be deliberately altered through the application of power, in the form of threats or sanctions. The process by which applied power inadvertently contributes to a losses frame, the contexts in which this is more or less likely, and the magnitude of such effects remain open questions and therefore fruitful avenues for future empirical research. One important consequence highlighted here is that the application of power can inadvertently contribute to a losses frame, motivating unwanted behavior. Prospect theory thus forces a distinction between credible threats and the effective use of power. The two may not always be the same. Credible threats that create a losses frame produce risk acceptance. In military affairs, this manifests in aggressive attempts to overrun the status quo. In economic affairs, this also means pursuing a risky strategy whereby a state tenaciously refuses to alter its policies. Additionally, attempts at altering behavior through sanctions will similarly find frustration by the risk-acceptant intransigence to the extent to which they contribute to a losses frame.

Chapter 4

Cooperation

INTRODUCTION

Perhaps the most significant contribution of rational choice theory to the study of interstate cooperation is the identification of dilemmas wherein incentives drive actors away from cooperation even though all are better off if cooperation is observed. Such conditions are vexing: decision makers desire greater cooperation but are propelled by utility maximization into unilateral strategies. In the study of international relations, scholars rightly point to incentive dilemmas as an important area for study because their resolution represents a significant step toward increased and more effective interstate collaboration.

Under rational choice, a necessary condition for cooperation is the belief that there is more to be gained from collaboration than from unilateralism. Prospect theory adds to this an understanding that decision maker evaluations of the status quo—the decision frame—will also powerfully shape strategies related to cooperation. Rather than a complete review, the discussion here focuses upon two prominent incentive structures: the prisoner's dilemma and the tragedy of the commons. Beginning with these simple but common structures is the necessary first step toward the full formal expression of a cognitive theory of cooperation.

PROPOSITIONS ON NEGOTIATION AND COOPERATION

Often, the most significant hurdle to cooperation between states involves securing an initial commitment to negotiate. Negotiations involve risk because they require commitment to a process in which the outcome is uncertain. Governments often prefer an initial period of informal prenegotiation as a prelude. This minimizes both the uncertainties inherent in the process and the domestic audience costs of exiting. That is, prenegotiation can be attractive to states because it permits lower costs for exiting:

> The option to withdraw remains open, and leaders can exercise that option before domestic political interests have had the opportunity to organize and mobilize, either on behalf of or against negotiation. Prenegotiation is usually a less public process than is negotiation and interested outsiders have less access to critical information. [Prenegotiation] is better insulated from political interests and, in this sense too, leaders can acquire critical information at lower cost. The political costs of information are less at the outset of prenegotiation than in negotiation. (Stein 1989, 274)[1]

The exit costs associated with abandoning negotiations, combined with the fact that the eventual outcome is ultimately unknown, means that the decision to enter into negotiations constitutes a gamble. Prospect theory thus predicts that states in a losses frame are more likely to accept the risks inherent in formal negotiations than states in a gains frame. Laboratory experiments on negotiations between individuals confirm this prediction (Bottom 1998). Actors pursue negotiation even when they expect that they will likely have to absorb the additional costs of failure, so long as negotiation promises some small chance of producing an acceptable status quo.

This raises a seeming paradox: if negotiation is a gamble, then we would expect very few successful agreements. Risk-acceptant states operating in a losses frame would constantly call for new political settlements, while gains frame states, not wanting to undertake new risks, would simply ignore them. Yet negotiations often succeed. As chapter 2 demonstrated, it is possible for states to simultaneously view the status quo as unacceptable. In addition, recall from the discussion of renormalization that losses are more slowly incorporated into an updated reference point than gains. It is therefore possible for two states to simultaneously view themselves to be in a losses frame when, in fact, only one actually suffers under current conditions. Under such circumstances, states will adopt risk-acceptant strategies and are therefore more apt to gamble on negotiation.

The notion that negotiation constitutes a risk-acceptant strategy is obviously not accurate in cases where all the alternatives to negotiation are more costly. Here, negotiation would represent a strategy of minimizing losses. Also, states pursue negotiations for a variety of motives. The onset of a losses frame for participants is then not a necessary condition for serious negotiations to commence. Prospect theory does, however, identify this as a new factor promoting the onset of negotiations even when an expected benefits calculation leads governments to expect that the endeavor will fail.

Cooperation can also be risky. Often, the motive to seek cooperation emerges from an understanding by all parties that the noncooperative status quo is undesirable. When cooperation risks still further losses, but also promises some chance of improving conditions, it can constitute a risky strategy. Under prospect theory, states in a losses frame are more likely to pursue risky cooperation than are states in a gains frame.[2] The idea that states cooperate to avoid loss is not new. Under rational choice, states will select cooperation if that strategy minimizes expected losses. The argument under prospect theory is instead that governments operating under a losses frame will eschew the "smaller but certain losses from defection" in favor of the "larger but uncertain losses from cooperation" (Stein and Pauly 1993, 22).

While such decisions stand in direct contrast to the behavioral expectations of classic rationality, there is empirical evidence that governments opt for risky cooperation even if they expect further loss from the attempt. In its pursuit of the Structural Impediments Initiative (discussed in chapter 2), the United States framed the status quo as a loss. Decision makers viewed the successful conclusion of the initiative as a risky venture that implied further costs but also provided some small chance of minimizing existing political and economic losses. Here, the onset of a losses frame made cooperation easier to achieve than rationality would permit because U.S. policymakers were willing to accept a level of risk under a losses frame that would be unacceptable under utility maximization. By contrast, in a gains frame, states are risk averse and therefore less likely to pursue a strategy of cooperation. Governments will eschew cooperation that they expect will be profitable whenever such cooperation promises larger uncertain gains beyond the smaller certain gains under the status quo.

During negotiation, each government will treat its own concessions as losses while treating rival concessions as gains. Given an asymmetrical value function in which losses are weighted more heavily than equivalent gains, even if both states grant concessions of objectively equal value, each will nonetheless perceive that it made greater concessions. Levy notes that this creates important but understudied hurdles to successful cooperation in the form of a concession aversion that essentially shrinks the bargaining space of mutually beneficial exchanges, produces a greater tendency to risk the consequences of nonagreement, and thus decreases the probability of negotiated agreement below that which a utility-based bargaining theory would predict (Levy 1996, 187).

Political subjectivity therefore can be as important in shaping decision frames as objective payoffs—a point made earlier but worth reiterating here. A subjectively constructed frame—where only perception is operative regardless of objective circumstances—is consistent with Kahneman and Tversky's finding that "the reference point is [sometimes] determined by events that are only imagined" (Kahneman and Tversky 1982, 171–72). The process of frame creation—that is, the process by which value is attached to the status quo—is an empirical issue. Prospect theory cannot predict the reference point for a decision. Changes in state leadership, the influence of important domestic political actors, or the dissemination of new information, as well as changes in objective structures, can lead to the constitution or redefinition of a decision frame. The point here is that two states looking at the same set of structures can have quite different perspectives on the attractiveness of the status quo and therefore on the desirability of proposed cooperation.

Prospect theory thus argues that cooperation will be both easier and more difficult than rational choice suggests, depending upon each state's assessment of the status quo. States in a gains frame will decline cooperation—even when they expect successful cooperation to produce further gains—whenever there is some risk to existing benefits. States in a losses frame will choose to cooperate even when cooperation has an expected outcome of loss, so long as it also provides some small probability of improving conditions.

These propositions may at first seem counterintuitive. At the outset, I suggested that there is value in exploring the logic of prospect theory even if some of the results are unsatisfactory, so that we can better understand the scope of issues to which the framework might be usefully applied. However, the sections below suggest that once these general propositions are integrated into existing international relations theory, they no longer seem improbable. In fact, they produce intuitively appealing results. The remainder of this chapter examines common incentive dilemmas using the argument I've just outlined. Traditionally, incentive dilemmas attempt to capture the essential character of international politics through rationalist analysis. My analysis begins instead with prospect theory. The result reveals a new set of conditions that are required for successful cooperation and uncovers a new set of reasons for cooperative failure that run counter to conventional understanding. From these findings follow a new set of policy prescriptions for states wishing to craft stable cooperative relationships.

COOPERATION AND THE PRISONER'S DILEMMA

The analytic power of game theory derives from generalized incentive structures that reflect a broad set of choice dilemmas confronting states. The strength in this approach for the study of international politics lies in its capacity to simultaneously integrate anarchic interaction, cooperation, and conflict under a single deductive rubric. The most widely studied incentive structure is the prisoner's dilemma (PD). Increasingly, research outside political science establishes the influence of prospect theory over individuals attempting to fashion cooperation under conditions of social dilemma,[3] yet little if any notice of this work exists among students of international politics. The purpose of this chapter is to develop a framework for the study of state behavior under social dilemma conditions.

The standard PD has states facing the choice set given in figure 4.1. Here, unilateral cooperation is the least attractive outcome. The next best option is mutual defection, and then mutual cooperation. The dominating strategy is defection; defection is best no matter the choice of the other player. If all play this strategy, the suboptimal outcome represented by the payoffs in the mutual defection cell results.

Liberal analysis has demonstrated that governments overcome the incentive to defect by restructuring the interaction.[4] Decomposing difficult problems into many (smaller) discrete decisions promotes cooperation to the extent that it creates an iterated game among rational agents who play conditionally cooperative strategies: for example, tit-for-tat (Axelrod 1984). In this context, international institutions promote cooperation in several ways. Most importantly, they provide participants with information about the actions of other states (Krasner 1983). Information is a necessary condition for playing conditional strategies and thus also for cooperation. Institutions also clearly define cheating and identify legitimate verification and monitoring procedures (Stein 1983, 129). This reduces transaction costs and permits governments to cooperate free from the fear of hidden exploitation by others. Decentralized or individualized information gathering outside formal institutions is by contrast less efficient (Kydd and Snidal 1993, 118) and inhibits cooperation because governments, lacking accurate information about rival behavior, are less willing to cooperative themselves. Institutions also legitimate norms permitting group sanctioning against rogue states.

IS COOPERATION RISKY OR SAFE?

The answer to this question, of course, is that cooperation can be either risky or safe. As a result, decision frames significantly influence choices concerning cooperation. Risk in a PD is traditionally defined by the interaction of two factors. The first is the likelihood that partners will defect given one's own cooperation. If the probability of rival defection is high, cooperation is risky. Cooperation becomes safer as the probability of rival defection decreases. As noted above, one of the roles assigned by liberals to international institutions is verification, and to the extent that regimes help make behavior transparent,

	State A	
	Cooperate	Defect
State B Cooperate	6, 6	3, 7
State B Defect	7, 1	4, 4

FIGURE 4.1. Standard prisoner's dilemma game
Cooperation opens state A to more costly exploitation.

they reduce the risks of cooperating. The second source of risk is found in comparing matrix payoffs across games. For example, the incentive structure in figure 4.1 is riskier for state A because cooperation leaves that government open to a more costly form of exploitation.[5]

The willingness of governments to cooperate is thus largely dependent upon their confidence that rivals will reciprocate, which is itself a function of the quality of information available to participants. This suggests a third source of risk related to the reality of imperfect information that plagues any attempt to fashion cooperation under anarchy. Governments have opportunities to enter into both new and established institutions. Cooperation in new agreements leaves states more vulnerable to rival defection because participants have not demonstrated their desire or capacity to reciprocate, and institutions designed to support compliance are similarly untested. Regardless of the absolute payoffs in the matrix, cooperation in new relationships is thus risky compared to cooperation within the context of existing agreements where partners have solid reputations for cooperation and where institutions have proven themselves capable of effectively monitoring behavior. By contrast, defection is the risky strategy in established institutions. Iteration, conditionally cooperative strategies, and effective monitoring by international institutions provide powerful incentives promoting compliance, and the transparency created by a time-tested institution deters defection. Undetected cheating promises benefits above those produced by the cooperative status quo, but it also risks sanctions or expulsion from a profitable collective. As the probability of undetected defection is lower and the costs from undermining a productive relationship are greater, cooperation is the risk-averse strategy here.

Prospect theory therefore predicts that states confronted with a PD are more likely to accept the risks inherent in fashioning new cooperative arrangements when operating under a losses frame, and less likely to accept those same risks in a gains frame. Alternatively, states in a losses frame are more likely to risk defection within established cooperation than are states in a gains frame.

STRATEGIC CHOICE

To highlight the differences between rational game theory and prospect theory, compare figures 4.1 and 4.2. While both matrices are a PD, they depict different decision maker assessments about the acceptability of the status quo: figure 4.1 represents a gains frame and 4.2 a losses frame.[6] Assuming classic rationality, this difference is unimportant and we would expect states in the two games to act in an identical manner and consistent with a traditional interpretation of the payoffs. For example, states in established cooperative relationships with robust institutions will continue cooperation in either game so long as the future benefits of cooperation carry sufficient value and institutions fulfill their compliance-monitoring function. While decision makers may view the cooperate-cooperate outcome as less than ideal, as in figure 4.2, there is no incentive to disrupt the status quo when the likely outcome of defection brings sanctions, expulsion from the collective, or the dissolution of cooperation altogether.

By contrast, under prospect theory decision maker tolerance for risk is affected by the decision frame, and this produces different behavior in each game. Within established institutions, decision makers in figure 4.2 must choose between an unacceptable status quo and the benefits made possible through undetected defection. Continuing in the status quo produces the certain losses of the upper right quadrant. Defection risks still further losses because cooperation is supported by robust institutions; but, if undetected, this strategy can largely mitigate existing losses. This is a classic losses frame choice, and prospect theory predicts a greater tolerance for the risks attendant to defection. States in figure 4.1 operate under a gains frame and are also confronted with two choices. Decision makers must choose between an acceptable status quo and the increased benefits made possible through undetected cheating. While cheating promises still greater benefits if it succeeds, it is also risky because the cooperative arrangement is well established and the payoff from

	State A	
	Cooperate	Defect
State B Cooperate	-3, -3	-6, -2
Defect	-2, -6	-5, -5

FIGURE 4.2. Prisoner's dilemma game for states in a losses frame

getting caught less attractive than the status quo. Decision makers in this gains frame are risk adverse, less willing to risk losing the benefits under the status quo, and therefore more likely to continue cooperation.

While decision makers in a losses frame are more likely to defect within established cooperative relationships, because they are risk acceptant, such governments will therefore also energetically pursue new agreements. Risk acceptance means that decision makers are less likely to be deterred by the insecurity born from their concern about the opportunities for partner defection. Governments operating under a losses frame are therefore more likely to pursue new cooperation than when they operate under a gains frame. By contrast, rational choice demands that states first settle upon assurances that cheating can be identified, regardless of the decision frame. In part, this requires the creation of new institutional arrangements as a protection against undetected defection. States operating in the domain of losses will, however, accept greater risks in their attempt to secure an acceptable status quo. They are therefore more likely to accept less than adequate verification schemes in a push to get an agreement. Traditional rationalist analysis also predicts that states may cooperate in order to limit expected losses. By contrast, the argument here is that risk-acceptant states will chase cooperation even when rival noncompliance presents the possibility of still further losses.

If states in a losses frame are both more likely to risk initial cooperation for new agreements and defection in established agreements, new cooperation would be quickly undone by the risk-acceptant behavior of states in a losses frame. But we know that cooperation does in fact endure. States beginning in the noncooperative lower right cell of a PD game have two choices: accept the losses in the status quo, or attempt to fashion a new cooperative arrangement. While both may find current conditions to be unacceptable, attempting to fashion new cooperation is risky because it leaves states open to costly exploitation. However, the act of creating new cooperation reduces losses, thus producing a new status quo that represents an improvement over the old arrangement. Compared to the old status quo, new conditions represent a gain. Such states now shift to a gains frame and become risk averse. As noted above, this makes the newly established cooperative effort all the more robust.

The insights from prospect theory thus also offer a new perspective on the role played by international institutions. Under liberal analysis, successful cooperation is the result of properly crafted regimes (Mitchell 1994). If states desire cooperation they will pursue agreements when the verification provided by institutions is adequate. Prospect theory adds to this a new source of regime failure unrelated to traditionally conceived regime functions. Decision makers in a losses frame are risk acceptant and often select nonmaximizing strategies. The success of institutions is then largely dependent upon the decision frames of the participant states. A regime that effectively promotes cooperation while states are in a gains frame will be challenged if one or more members slip into a losses frame, regardless of its capacity to fulfill the functions deemed important by traditional theory. That is, governments will risk cheating even with an otherwise effective institution in place.

While the traditional interpretation of PD interactions also identifies compelling incentives to defect, the mechanism described here is different. Risk acceptance implies that governments will defect within existing agreements at rates higher than rationalist analysis predicts, and even when verification is good. Redrafting regime rules in order to create a more robust or intrusive institution is not a remedy for this sort of noncompliance, as implied by conventional liberal theory. Instead, successful institutions will be those that also affect decision makers' tolerance for risk by influencing the content of the decision frame. Shifting from the domain of losses to gains, or continual support for a gains frame, produces risk-averse behavior which, in established relationships with well-crafted institutions (in the conventional sense) diminishes the likelihood of defection. The utilization of rewards as incentives in creating or supporting a gains frame remains an important but little-studied function of institutions. While not a substitute for monitoring, a gains frame is an important condition for monitoring to serve as a meaningful constraint on noncompliance.

Finally, this argument contains implications for the ongoing debate between advocates of inducements versus sanctions as the best strategy for producing compliance in incentive dilemmas (e.g., Wettstad 1999, ch. 2). The idea behind incentives is to entice continued cooperation, while the purpose behind sanctions is to discipline rogue states into cooperative behavior. Again, rational choice is largely indifferent between the two strategies. Sanctions produce cooperation if the punishment costs are greater than the expected benefits of continued defection, while inducements produce cooperation if they outweigh the expected benefits of cheating. The likely reason for both this debate and the fact that it has not yet been resolved is that under rationalist theory, neither strategy eliminates the new underlying cause of defection identified here: high tolerance for risk under conditions of loss.

In a PD, actors improve their position through undetected cheating whether inducements or sanctions are deployed. In contrast, under prospect theory, the choice between sanctions and inducements has additional consequences not traditionally recognized as important. Both carrots and sticks can shape the content of a decision frame, but their effects will be quite different. Inducements, to the extent that they create or reinforce a gains frame and produce risk-adverse behavior will render defection an unattractive strategy because it represents unacceptable risks. As outlined above, defection can be risky within the context of established cooperation because it threatens a productive relationship. Sanctions, to the extent that they create or reinforce a losses frame, produce risky behavior. Pursuing undetected defection remains an attractive strategy so long as it promises even a small chance of returning to an acceptable condition.

Under rationalist theory, neither incentives nor sanctions will affect behavior if cheating remains undetected. However, states will alter their behavior if cheating represents unacceptable risks. Under prospect theory, inducements are therefore clearly superior to sanctions. To the extent that inducements produce or reinforce a gains frame, states become risk averse and opt for the certain gains under the cooperative status quo; even if defection promises still greater benefits. Ultimately, compliance with agreements is greater when states desire cooperation. Strategies deliberately designed to manipulate the decision frame through inducements are therefore more likely to produce stable cooperation over time.

This is not to suggest that rationalist explanations are wholly incorrect. Indeed, monitoring, side payments, punishment, and inducements all constitute effective tools in securing and sustaining cooperation. However, the success and failure of institutions is also heavily dependent upon the decision frame for each issue. The contribution of prospect theory is that it identifies this new contextual factor that both supports and undermines traditional regime functions.

There are obviously many more incentive structures in international politics than can be considered here, and the application of game theory to international relations goes well beyond the metaphor of a prisoner's dilemma. The logic for state choice according to prospect theory would be different for each game structure, and different than traditional rationalist theory posits. Disputes with rational game theory, where they exist, should be articulated in full so that students of international politics gain a comprehensive sense of the implications of prospect theory in game theoretic analysis. Here, narrowly considering only the prisoner's dilemma, prospect theory suggests an alternative set of dynamics governing the formation and dissolution of cooperation. States in a losses frame are more willing to cheat in established cooperative relationships than rational choice suggests, and such states are also more inclined to risk new cooperation. The traditional regime functions of coordination and monitoring are less effective for states under loss than they are for states operating under gains. This suggests that in addition to these functions, greater attention must be paid to states' tolerance for risk produced by their assessments of the status quo.

Cooperation and the Tragedy of the Commons

The international system is also populated by collective action problems in which states make individually rational choices that often generate collectively deficient outcomes.[7] Much of the discussion of prospect theory and PDs applies to the problem of collective action. Governments will accept greater risk under conditions of loss than under conditions of gain. As before, with new agreements the risk lies in contributing to the collective good while others do not. Free-riding, if it is widespread, damages the position of cooperators. In existing agreements—assuming effective institutions—cheating is risky to the extent that it raises the probability of sanctions or expulsion from the collective.

Under a losses frame, governments are more likely to initiate new cooperation than rational choice suggests, while such governments will also be more likely to risk cheating on an established agreement. States under a gains frame will be less likely to risk new agreements, and less likely to cheat within established cooperation.

Importantly, not all collective action problems are the same. Traditionally, scholars have not treated the distinction between public goods and commons protection to be an important one (e.g., Jervis 1988). Public goods require governments to make a contribution from existing endowments, while commons protection demands that they restrict consumption of an existing resource. The difference is largely unimportant in rationalist theory because actors treat the cost of contribution identically to the cost of forgoing gains. That is, it does not matter whether the cost involved is a payment or a new restriction on one's ability to consume. Governments therefore will be indifferent between the two forms of collective action, and we should find no difference in their ability to create and sustain cooperation across the two types.

By contrast, there is an emerging experimental literature demonstrating that the difference between contribution and restraint is an important distinction that affects decision maker choices.[8] These results are anchored to the findings, discussed earlier, that decision maker value functions are steeper in the domain of losses than in the domain of gains, and that through the endowment effect, actors demand more for something they already possess than they would be willing to pay to acquire it. One result of this is the so-called concession aversion noted earlier. Where two governments grant concessions of equal value, each will nonetheless perceive that it made the greater contribution. A compromise that is judged fair to an outside observer will appear to each participant as placing unfair demands upon it.

An additional consequence is that governments will behave differently when confronted with these two forms of collective action. It is harder for states to create and sustain cooperation in public goods treaties than in restraint agreements. Given loss aversion, and all other things being equal, the act of creating a public good is subjectively more expensive than an equal amount of restraint. Asking parties to contribute to a public good requires that they give up endowments they already possess. Such contributions are more likely to trigger the endowment effect because actors place greater value on the loss of goods possessed than upon the comparable cost of forgone gains, which are by definition not part of an existing endowment. Cooperation is therefore easier when it involves a choice not to take from the commons than when it requires real contributions to a public good.

The domestic impact of agreements is crucial here because domestic pressure groups in part define the nature of collective action. For example, restrictions on pollution seem a clear-cut example of restraint: governments agree not to deplete an ecosystem's capacity to absorb and process waste. Such restraint can also require a contribution, however, in the form of new facilities to reduce pollution. This cost is often imposed upon private sector polluters, requiring from them a real contribution. Likewise, if domestic actors treat the benefits of exploited commons as an endowment they possess, then restricting consumption can be reinterpreted as requiring a real contribution to the cooperative effort. The longer the benefits of commons consumption have been enjoyed, the more likely it is that such benefits will become viewed as an endowment. However, the intervening political process by which an act of restraint can be redefined as contribution will be unique to each case, as will the degree to which this occurs. The point here is that cooperation will be similarly difficult to achieve whether actors must make actual contribution or if they redefine an act of restraint as requiring a contribution.

This is not to suggest that public goods treaties are impossible. Indeed, both contribution and restraint treaties currently exist. For example, the 1993 Agreement to Promote Compliance with International Conservation and

Management Measures by Fishing Vessels on the High Seas closely resembles a restraint treaty. Overfishing reduces the supply of a resource available to others. Here, corrective action requires self-restraint. By contrast, the 1993 Convention of Biological Diversity requires, among other things, that developed states transfer technology and financial resources to developing states. This is best classified as a public goods instrument because corrective action requires direct payments to protect ecological diversity. The argument here is simply that a public goods compromise will be more difficult for governments to accept politically, in part because they will confront greater opposition to domestic ratification by affected groups.

Thus, both our empirical understanding of cooperation and public policy issues are relevant to the distinction between contribution and restraint cooperation unearthed by prospect theory. Most obviously, there are now compelling theoretical reasons to treat the two forms as distinct and therefore to begin an investigation into how this difference affects actual behavior. It also suggests that governments are well-served to understand the political consequences of the two forms. For example, in protecting renewable resources—fisheries, timber, and so on—states have two options. They can overharvest and agree to share the cost of regenerating the resource through direct contribution, or they may agree to create quotas to keep future consumption within naturally sustainable limits. While traditional theory is silent as to which form of cooperation is more likely to succeed, prospect theory suggests that the second strategy is more likely to meet with success because restraint agreements are more likely to elicit cooperative behavior.

Additionally, rationalist theory has established that the use of side payments to domestic groups is an effective way to blunt opposition to the costs of an international treaty (Mayer 1992; Petrakis 1996; Cameron 1997). The capacity of governments to distribute side payments is thus an important factor influencing the prospects for cooperation. Often, attempts at cooperation fail because states cannot agree on a scheme for sharing the burden of providing the resources sufficient for meaningful side payments. Because the subjective value attached to a given cost of restraint is lower than an equal cost of providing new public goods, the level of side payment required to overcome opposition to an agreement is less in restraint cooperation than in public goods treaties. States will therefore find it easier to marshal the necessary resources for side payments to the extent that they pursue restraint agreements.

Prospect theory thus adds to the logic of collective action a new set of theorems about the capacity of states to act collectively that emphasizes the finding of a loss aversion by decision makers. Commons cooperation is easier to achieve than public goods agreements. States should attempt restraint rather than contribution, when such a choice exists, because such agreements are easier for delegates to take home and sell to their domestic constituents. It is also possible that the true nature of an agreement will be redefined through domestic political debate as it is being considered for ratification, making cooperation more difficult.

CONCLUSION

Prospect theory and rational choice offer two very different views of the conditions conducive to cooperation. Rational choice asserts that states will cooperate when the net benefits of cooperation are greater than the net benefits of unilateralism. By contrast, prospect theory does not view the promise of further gains as a necessary condition for cooperation. Under loss, states are risk acceptant, and they will pursue a gamble with an expected outcome of greater loss if, in so doing, there is some prospect of mitigating losses. This means that states in a losses frame may seize on the opportunity to cooperate even when they expect that the attempt will fail. By contrast, states in a gains frame are risk averse and will forgo a gamble with an expected outcome of still further gain if they must risk the gains enjoyed under the status quo. Such states are therefore unlikely to risk new forms of cooperation. Thus, depending upon the decision frame, cooperation is both easier and more difficult than is suggested by rational choice.

This implies that conventional wisdom regarding the role of institutions in promoting cooperation requires some revision. The functions served by institutions are more effective when governments are in a gains frame than when they operate under conditions of loss. In addition, prospect theory forces an important distinction between the two forms of collective action: public goods and commons protection. Rational choice holds that governments are indifferent as to which strategy is adopted. In either case, decision makers simply weigh the costs and benefits of participation and make a maximizing choice. By contrast, prospect theory suggests that collective action organized around restraint is more likely to succeed than action requiring direct contribution. Where governments have a choice, they therefore should attempt to craft restraint treaties because they are more likely to meet with success.

The discussion of conflict and cooperation up to this point has governments pursuing generic gains or avoiding generic losses. Recently, scholars have argued that states do not pursue generic goals. Instead, states have a more subtle set of preferences. Liberals argue that states pursue absolute gains while realists assert that states chase relative position. The next chapter takes up this gains debate in detail. It demonstrates that the debate is itself a theoretical artifact inherent to the deployment of rational choice in the construction of international relations theory. Prospect theory is used to construct a new theoretical framework that explains both realist and liberal assumptions under a unified theory of preferences.

Chapter 5

A Unified Theory
of Preferences

INTRODUCTION

Previous chapters focused on states pursuing preexisting goals. This section takes up the task of explaining goals themselves. Rather than a direct contrast of rational choice and prospect theory, the purpose here is to sketch an independent model of state preferences. My focus is the so-called gains debate between realists and liberals that absorbed considerable intellectual energy during the 1990s. The debate is largely a theoretical artifact, deriving from a particular application of rational choice. After a brief summary and discussion of the origins of the gains debate, I offer a resolution grounded in prospect theory.[1] This model is then integrated into the discussion of conflict and cooperation presented in previous chapters.

THE GAINS DEBATE

The desire to understand the origins of state goals stems from the long-standing attempt to discern broader patterns in international behavior. After World War II, Morganthau's *Politics among Nations* (1960) helped cement realism's dominant position in the academy, and realist "assumptions about the world" quickly "dominated research and policymaking" in both the United States and Great Britain (Vasquez 1998, 38). However, in the mid-1980s liberal institutionalism challenged realism in a convincing way. Liberals accepted—indeed adopted—many realist arguments, including the importance of anarchy, the theoretical utility of state-centric decision units, and the assumption of rational decision making. Despite this appropriation of realist principles, liberal analysis offered greater optimism regarding the prospects for meaningful international collaboration and a much more prominent role for international institutions in promoting and sustaining cooperation. Liberal arguments proved compelling and spawned a decade-long investigation that challenged established realist doctrines. Realists responded by reasserting that the primary concern of all governments in international relations is domination by rivals. Therefore, liberal arguments regarding the central importance of absolute gains seeking by states were misguided. Rather than seeking mutually profitable interactions with others in order to improve their lot, realists argue that governments seek relative gains over rivals and partners. This controversy "dominated much of international relations theory" in the 1990s such that it was "commonplace" for research—whatever the substantive issue—to first locate itself in terms of this debate (Powell 1994, 313).

Both empirical and policy issues were at stake in this debate. For example, relative gains seeking implies that cooperation is only possible where the distribution of gains from cooperation does not produce meaningful changes in relative position, whatever the potential for absolute gains. In contrast, under liberalism, even those arrangements that produce changes in relative position can sustain cooperation so long as they also provide absolute gains. Under liberalism, institutions can enhance the prospects for cooperation to the extent that they help allay fears that partners will cheat—suggesting that the intelligent design of institutions can itself produce cooperation. Because realism emphasizes distributional issues, institutions are less effective: they do not possess the requisite power to ensure that the gains from cooperation are distributed in an equitable fashion.

Often, such debates produce important theoretical innovations in the form of unified approaches that adopt the strongest arguments from each side. Unfortunately, in the gains debate, polarization resulted and each side "failed to contribute as much as they might have to international relations theory" (Powell 1994, 313). Structured discussion between camps failed to produce consensus. If anything, the debate became increasingly discordant.[2] Ultimately, the participants tired of dialogue, remained convinced of their own arguments, and returned home to their respective research programs. The disagreement is now simply accepted as part of the contested theoretical terrain in the field (Walt 1998). The central issues in the dispute remain and continue to stimulate attempts at resolution (e.g., Jervis, 1999) and guide research in international relations and related fields.[3] Important issues remain unresolved; for example, realists and liberals still disagree over the importance of international institutions.

While the very need for such a debate is challenged by an empirical reality in which states exhibit behavior consistent with both approaches, the two sides of the debate remain largely unreconciled. Examples in which states switch between relative and absolute gains across issue areas—or switch between them within an issue area or during a single set of negotiations—confront both realist and liberal depictions and support the call for new integrative approaches that combine the predictions of both camps into a single coherent theory of state choice.

This chapter draws selectively from prospect theory in the construction of a unified theory of state goals. The argument is that states pursue absolute gains when in a gains frame and chase relative position when in a losses frame. Results from this chapter suggest that prospect theory provides an even more fertile ground for theory construction than has already been established. It also demonstrates that theoretical progress on the formation of state goals is possible by deploying alternatives to classic rationality.

THE PROBLEM OF FIXED PREFERENCES

The reformulation of traditional realism by Kenneth Waltz (1979) serves as the cornerstone for modern realism. Waltz pulled explanation from the unit state outward, into the international system. Here, anarchy defines the most relevant characteristic of international politics because it requires that states provide for their own security. As Waltz puts it:

> When faced with the possibility of cooperating for mutual gain, states that feel insecure must ask how the gain will be divided. They are compelled to ask not "Will both of us gain?" but "Who will gain more?" If an expected gain is to be divided, say, in the ratio of two to one, one state may use its disproportionate gain to implement a policy intended to damage or destroy the other. Even the prospect of large absolute gains for both parties does not elicit their cooperation so long as each fears how the other will use its increased capabilities. (Waltz 1979, 105)

Subsequent additions to the realist paradigm are even more explicit on this point. Emphasis is placed upon the "core insight" of realism that "states recognize that in anarchy there is no overarching authority to prevent others from using violence, or the threat of violence, to dominate or even destroy them" (Grieco 1990, 38). Vulnerability under anarchy produces a perpetual concern for survival, and states are therefore at all times concerned with their comparative position. Even if some states are not driven by greed or ambition, the continuous threat of war and domination imposes upon governments a strategy of survival through relative gains seeking.

In contrast, liberals argue that a world populated with international institutions voluntarily created between states is evidence that states prefer absolute gain, not relative position. The decision to cooperate under anarchy often resembles an n-person prisoner's dilemma. Mutual cooperation benefits all, but defectors or free riders achieve greater gains at the expense of cooperative states. The object of the game is to maximize one's own utility and "to do as well as possible, regardless of how well the other player does" (Axelrod 1984, 22). State utility functions are therefore "independent of one another" and states do not "gain or lose utility simply because of the gains or losses of others" (Keohane 1984, 27). Rather than a direct security threat, the compelling characteristic of anarchy is that it lacks any meaningful coordinating mechanism. The result is missed opportunities for mutual gain that can be recovered only through cooperation, but only if states pursue absolute gains. Because security concerns are de-emphasized, relative gains do not, and should not, restrict attempts to secure multilateral collaboration. States are absolute gains maximizers, seeking power, wealth, and military might while remaining largely indifferent to the circumstances of other states.

The realist charge (Grieco 1990, 39) that liberals see states as only concerned with well-being and not survival is overstated. It is consistent with liberalism to assert that states seek wealth and power because anarchy is a self-help system. That is, states are "dedicated to their own self-preservation, ultimately able to depend only on themselves" (Stein 1983, 116). Rather than pursue relative advantage, under liberalism states attempt to maximize their own returns in pursuit of security. Still, compared to realists, liberals do de-emphasize the survival imperative and instead see anarchy's defining feature in its lack of an institution or agency to establish and enforce rules of conduct. Without an authority to enforce rules, states can free ride on attempts to achieve gains through joint cooperation.

Despite their differences, the two perspectives are similar in one important respect. Both explicitly assume classic rationality as the state decision rule. This means that actor goals are exogenous. This requires that both realists and liberals prespecify state preferences. In order to produce a framework that offers systematic analysis, general theories like realism and liberalism require stable and consistent preferences across contexts. Indeed, as noted above, each camp takes as its primary task the establishment of a fixed set of goals deduced from the imperatives of anarchy. While they differ on what properly constitute the most relevant characteristics of anarchic systems—security concerns versus lack of coordination—both address the requirement for a stable set of preferences by arguing that such characteristics are permanent.

Unfortunately, there are no universally agreed upon anarchical imperatives. Even (seemingly) incontestable concepts like the lack of formal order under anarchy are disputed (Milner 1991; Schmidt 1998). Furthermore, recent constructivist arguments demonstrate that the imperatives of anarchy are neither inherent nor timeless, but are instead created by states themselves.[4] Contested interpretations of anarchy thus support both realist and liberal assumptions. As a result, neither realism nor liberalism can sustain the argument that state preferences are fixed to the permanent characteristics of anarchic systems.

For example, even a cursory examination of recent history would seem to side against a strong interpretation of realism. States have passed out of existence, but this is rare. Even when defeated in war, they are often allowed to continue—for example, Japan and Germany after World War II, Serbia in the 1990s, and so forth. While this challenges the premise that states are permanently threatened, the ardent realist might respond that the endurance of states is a direct result of their attentiveness to the pernicious imperatives of anarchy. It is because of their concern for relative gains that states endure. However, this means that the insecurity of anarchy can be overcome. Once sufficient defenses are in place, governments can free themselves from concern for the capacities and intentions of others. The explanation for a relative gains preference is then not anarchy but context. In contexts in which a state's defenses are sufficient to ensure survival, there is no need to pursue relative gains at the expense of other goals.

An alternative construction of realism could argue that no matter the actual threat to states in anarchy, all states—even secure ones—nonetheless interpret anarchy as threatening. States pursue relative gains because they see in anarchy the potential for their undoing—even if it is in reality unlikely. However, this suggests that there can exist a fundamental discontinuity between the reality of anarchy and government perceptions of it. While states are not actually threatened with extinction, they nonetheless worry, for example, that "today's friend may be tomorrow's enemy in war" (Grieco 1990, 28–29). Here the explanation for relative gains preference is not anarchy, but rather the perception of threat. Perception is malleable, and realism provides no reason to expect a consistent adherence to the mistaken view that states are threatened in those contexts in which they are not. If it were to do so, realism would cast off its theoretic core to embrace misperception, experience, history, context, and ideology—to the extent that they impact decision maker world views—as central to explaining preferences.

On the origin of preferences, contemporary liberalism suffers under a different but related problem. The liberal assertion is that the decision to cooperate often resembles a prisoner's dilemma, and therefore that observed cooperation reveals a preference for absolute gains. However, state behavior in any given incentive structure is not sufficient evidence for asserting a specific gains preference.[5] Under rationalist theory, goals do not derive from the incentive-compatible solution unique to each social dilemma game; they predate it. While noncooperation can be the result of weak institutions, as liberals often claim, unsuccessful attempts to secure cooperation can also derive from irreconcilable state preferences. If states primarily care about "maximizing their power advantage and not about absolute gains and losses, many of the strategies and conditions that should lead to cooperation in a prisoner's dilemma no longer produce this result" (Jervis 1978, 334). Axelrod himself notes that a concern for relative gains leads to "conflict" and the breakdown of cooperation (Axelrod 1984, 111). Given simply state behavior, it is theoretically impossible to distinguish between irreconcilable preferences and free riding as the reason for failed attempts at cooperation.

The gains debate is, then, an artifact owing largely to the requirement under rational choice for prespecified preferences. Attempting to derive a single set of universal goals that logically emerge from anarchic systems represents a flawed strategy for theory construction. The resultant bifurcation of international relations theory into competing schools means that neither approach alone is capable of grasping the actual breadth of state choice. That governments appear to exhibit behavior consistent with both realism and liberalism is additional reason to pursue a unified theory of preferences.

Constructivism and the Gains Debate

Constructivism currently enjoys increasing popularity in international relations and therefore deserves mention as a potential resolution to the debate between realism and liberalism. While it has not yet been applied to the gains debate—its ascendence began after the debate had cooled—it is not difficult to derive a constructivist explanation for a relative or absolute gains preference. Constructivism holds that state behavior is conditioned by (usually elite) norms and identities, and that such norms and identities are transmitted through social discourse. Ultimately, the physical world is "given meaning only by the social context" through which it is interpreted (Checkel 1998, 326). Constructivists are thus skeptical of the methodological individualism inherent to rational choice or prospect theory. They are also explicitly critical of the neorealist/neoliberal dichotomy in international relations theory. Neither theory adequately accounts for the formation of identities and interests that are the foundation for all governmental choices and action (Checkel 1998).

Under this view, preferences are not inherent in anarchic systems; they are constructed through social practice. As Wendt (1992) famously notes in his response to traditional theory, anarchy is simply "what states make of it," rather than the foundation for a single universal set of preferences. An appetite for relative or absolute gains is, then, a function of the dominant discourses regarding security, wealth, and who one's friends or enemies are. For example, Wendt describes the remaking of Soviet identity under Gorbachev, whereby Russia began to view itself less as a rival and more as a partner with the West. We would expect that as this new identity solidified, Russia would be decreasingly worried about relative position and more attracted by opportunities for absolute gains in cooperation with the West. These identities and interests have continued to evolve as the relationship between Russia and the West has recently soured. We should therefore expect a reemergence of a security-oriented identity and a concomitant increased appetite for relative gains. In sum, as identities change so do interests, and this produces new gains preferences.

The advantage of this approach over realist and liberal theory is that constructivism not only permits states to pursue both relative and absolute gains—something traditional theory cannot—it also offers an explanation for the process by which preferences change. However, two shortcomings limit the capacity of the approach to satisfactorily resolve the debate. First, constructivism contains little predicative power beyond currently established discursive settlements. By definition, constructivism cannot predict how state identities and interests will evolve (Walt 1998). It can at best observe such changes, and then trace backwards through time to uncover the set of practices by which the current discursive settlement emerged. Second, while the shared norms, identities, and interests that are the objects of constructivist theory and that produce a particular gains preference evolve, they are not generally prone to radical departures. Indeed, as startling as it was, even the redefinition of Russia by Gorbachev was years in the making and required not just one individual's new perspective, but also a set of social-structural dynamics upon which Gorbachev capitalized. The approach is thus pressed to explain rapid changes in gains preference because the discursive dynamics underlying preference are slow to change. Actual state behavior often exhibits such radical shifts in preference; the European Community behavior discussed in chapter 6 is an example. While constructivism is a better fit with actual state behavior than traditional theory in that it permits states to pursue both relative and absolute gains, it is still empirically challenged in that it remains less flexible than actual state practice.

UNIFYING PREFERENCES

One could begin by simply adopting existing realist and liberal assumptions regarding goals and then substitute prospect theory for classic rationality. For states seeking relative gains, prospect theory provides two predictions. First, if a state declines relative to a rival, it will prefer a risky strategy to regain the distance lost—even if the expected outcome is further relative decline over the new status quo. Second, if a state gains relative to a rival, it will opt for the status quo over a gamble with an expected outcome of further relative gain. Alternatively, a state may prefer absolute over relative gains. Here again, there are two predictions. First, when the state experiences absolute losses, it will opt for a gamble over the status quo even if the expected outcome is further loss, so long as the gamble also contains some probability of returning to an acceptable condition. Second, when a state experiences absolute gains, it will opt for the new status quo over a risky strategy with an expected outcome of further absolute gain.

In traditional realist and liberal theory, states seek relative or absolute gains whenever the expected benefits outweigh the expected costs. Prospect theory goes beyond this to explain when and why states forgo maximizing their preferences. States will not maximize in a gains frame due to risk aversion, and in a losses frame they will accept inordinate risk. This may itself justify further investigation. However, we are still left without an important requirement for a new unified theory of state preferences—a logic that permits us to predict when states will exhibit a preference for relative or absolute gains.

The Importance of Leverage

Attempts to resolve the gains debate have focused upon the issue of leverage. States are compelled by relative position when the concern for rival leverage is manifest and are free to pursue absolute gains when the fear of rival leverage is diminished. Two prominent attempts are discussed here. While each is incomplete, together they offer a point of entry for integrating prospect theory into a model of leverage that, in turn, will move us toward a resolution of the gains debate.

Snidal offers a model under which realist arguments are compelling "only in the very special case of the two-state interaction, with high concern for relative gains and near disregard for absolute gains" (1991, 701). Essentially, the model substitutes a more flexible depiction of state preferences for rigid liberal and realist assumptions. Whenever there are more than two states involved, relative gains seeking does not inhibit cooperation even if gains are unequally distributed because leverage concerns are distributed across potential rivals; that is, "as the number of states goes up, . . . relative gains concerns must now be distributed across more states" (Snidal 1993a, 739). When the number of rivals increases beyond two, the impact of relative gains on state behavior is sharply attenuated such that cooperation is 'no more difficult then under pure absolute gains-seeking' (Snidal 1993a:739). This places severe restrictions on the contexts in which realist insights adhere, elevating the importance of liberal analysis.

While greater flexibility is given here to state preferences than is traditionally permitted, it is possible to construct simple counterexamples that undermine the model. Imagine three states considering joint cooperation. States A and B are powerful and rivals, with A just slightly more powerful than B. C is weak relative to both A and B. Assume as well that the distribution of gains from proposed cooperation is as follows: A receives one additional unit, and B and C receive four units each.[6] The logic of Snidal's model implies that, from the perspective of A, the relative gain of three units by both B and C is equally troubling. But if the concern for relative position derives at least in part from a fear of rival capacities, it is reasonable to expect that A is less threatened by C's gain than by B's. To carry this point further, assume that prior to cooperation, A's endowments surpassed B's by two units. We should therefore expect that A would be quite concerned with its new postcooperation position behind B, and therefore that A will decline the offer to join in cooperation. The model thus significantly underestimates the influence of relative gains seeking because it cannot sufficiently differentiate between contexts in which states view rival leverage as threatening from those in which they do not.

Powell's (1991) attempt couches the issue differently. The goal here is to determine when states will continue cooperating even if the gains from cooperation are distributed unequally. Here, states make assessments about the threat of leverage based upon status quo assets. Cooperation is possible so long as the unequal distribution offers neither state an advantage that can be used as leverage in the next round of interaction. The model qualifies liberalism in that "cooperative outcomes that offer unequal absolute gains can not be an equilibrium in the system" if, as a result of such gains, a rival secures a strategic advantage over its partner (Powell 1991, 1316). However, states will continue to cooperate so long as rival relative gains have no bearing upon the state's ability to pursue its own smaller absolute gains in the next round. Once it becomes possible for the unequal gains from one round to be used as leverage in the next, states become acutely concerned with their relative position. Unfortunately, Powell's discussion is limited to the consideration of military breakthrough technologies. The assertion that states become threatened when rivals achieve a compelling military advantage is uncontroversial, and the possibility that a similar dynamic applies in contexts where the use of military force is not an issue remains unexplored.

In both of these models, relative gains concerns are, at least in part, contextual. Most versions of realist analysis would agree. Governments treat allies differently than rivals, and currently weak states are not as threatening to rivals as the currently powerful. As Grieco puts is, each state's "coefficient of sensitivity to gaps in payoffs can vary but is always greater than zero" (Grieco 1990, 41).

Leverage concerns are therefore derivative by nature. There can be no change in relative position without some change in absolute position. The opposite is not true: states may pursue relative gains but they do so by attempting to alter their own or rival absolute gains. While they disagree over the sufficient conditions, the two models discussed here also acknowledge that there are contexts in which states need not fear leverage and are therefore free to pursue absolute gains. The core issue is the emergence of leverage gained as a result of the unequal distribution of absolute gains that are the outcome of interaction. The resolution of the gains debate is to be found, then, in identifying a general rule for strategic and nonstrategic contexts in which governments view changes in absolute position as posing the threat of leverage.

Prospect Theory and Leverage

According to prospect theory, states will be more threatened by their own absolute decline than by rival absolute gains. That is, loss itself can trigger a concern about leverage and therefore about relative position. Recall that losses derive an exaggerated "sting" and are measured against a reference point, not an actor's net-asset position. This produces the asymmetry observed in the s-shaped value function discussed earlier. Because the function for losses is steeper than for gains, losses are comparatively overvalued. When experiencing decline in absolute payoffs, governments overvalue such losses. In making comparative assessments, policymakers will therefore overestimate the importance of rival relative gains produced as a result.[7]

That is, because losses hurt more than gains feel good, prospect theory tells us that states will be threatened more by their own absolute decline than by equal rival accomplishments. While an absolute loss "might be minor compared to a state's overall position . . . because it is evaluated with respect to the current reference point rather than one's new asset position, its effects tend to be evaluated in absolute rather than relative (to total assets) terms" (Levy 1992, 287). This means that the actual (absolute) level of loss need not be large compared to the state's overall position for it to produce leverage concerns. Indeed, "the very fact of a loss is often more important than the magnitude of the loss," and "large losses may not be that much worse than smaller ones" (Levy 1992, 287). In turn, this suggests that the threshold required for triggering concerns about rival leverage—that is, the amount of loss at which states become concerned with relative gains—is quite low and, in some circumstances, just the fact of decline is itself sufficient.

Given the heightened sensitivity to leverage under a losses frame, if we assume only that states make accurate assessments of the importance of changes in relative position under gains, we can predict that states are more concerned with relative gains in a losses frame than in a gains frame. However, prospect theory suggests that governments will not make accurate assessments about changes in relative position under a gains frame. The logic for gains is essentially the opposite of that for losses. The endowment effect discussed earlier finds that actors overvalue that which they possess and, therefore, that states overvalue the worth of their own accomplishments. The effects of this heuristic are compelling as the overvaluation of achieved gains is often quite large. This suggests that states experiencing absolute gains will underestimate any improvement in relative position experienced by a rival gaining more rapidly. Just as there exists an exaggerated attention to losses under a losses frame, in the gains frame, there exists a similar exaggeration of absolute gains that delays a concern about increasing rival leverage. With a diminished sensitivity to actual relative decline, governments are liberated to pursue absolute gains under the illusion of freedom from rival leverage.

The unequal distribution of absolute gains is therefore not an impediment to cooperation, as realism argues, if participant states are in a gains frame. Under gains, states overvalue their own accomplishments and underestimate changes in a rival's relative position. It is here that liberal arguments about the need for increasing the transparency of state behavior and reducing transaction costs will prove most effective in overcoming the incentive to defect under conditions of social dilemma, and will therefore also effectively promote and sustain cooperation. However, under a losses frame, realist analysis is superior because, under these conditions, leverage concerns and relative gains seeking will undermine attempts to secure cooperation. Because of leverage concerns, a state operating under a losses frame will not accept offers to cooperate, whatever the potential for absolute gains, whenever the distribution of absolute gains is unfavorable. It is important to note, however, that because states in a losses frame are also risk acceptant, they may pursue cooperation as a relative gains strategy—even when the prospects for success are small—so long as cooperation contains some chance of returning to an acceptable relative position.

Prospect theory thus allows for a synthesis of realist and liberal assumptions about state preferences. Rather than assert universalistic goals across contexts, the depiction here is that states are "prudent maximizers." They pursue absolute gains whenever possible, but are also concerned with external threats to sovereignty and therefore act to shield themselves against the possibility of leverage. Under an acceptable status quo, governments adopt conservative policies and are primarily motivated by absolute gains. However, states are also quick to act if current conditions change and the status quo is no longer beneficial. Here, states will accept greater risks and chase relative position in order to shield themselves against the possibility of leverage and return to an acceptable condition. Put succinctly, states in a gains frame pursue absolute gains and are risk averse, whereas states in a losses frame chase relative gains and are risk acceptant.

Rather than fixed and immutable, state goals are fluid and partially contingent upon the actions of others. This aspect of state behavior troubles participants in gains debate. Both realist and liberal perspectives offer generalized explanations of preference, but neither permits states to change their preferences. This fluidity in state preference also undercuts constructivist claims that gains preferences are solely a function of established discourses about norms for appropriate behavior and state interests. Prospect theory offers an explanation of state preferences that is context bound, rather than deduced from characteristics supposedly inherent to the international system. It can also explain and predict rapid shifts in gains preferences, a failing in construtivist approaches.

POWER, PREFERENCES, AND STRATEGIES

This use of prospect theory also suggests dimensions to power additional to those discussed in chapter 3. That chapter demonstrated that the application of power—through the deployment of threats or rewards—can establish a new decision frame or alter an existing frame. To the extent that the application of power changes the decision frame, it also changes the state's gains preference. The idea that power is useful in delimiting rival choice sets or getting rivals to negotiate in good faith has a venerable tradition. However, the assumption has traditionally been that the goals of targeted states remain unchanged when confronted with coercion, even if the current distribution of power denies the possibility of achieving them. The argument developed here adds to this the finding that an unintended consequence of the successful application of power—to the extent that it alters the decision frame—can also alter the content of targeted states' goals.

Assessments of the status quo may change quickly for any number of reasons, and the application of power can have an immediate impact. The use of threats, sanctions, or positive incentives transforms the implications of the status quo for the target of power. Under the framework outlined here, we would expect a concomitant shift in gains preference consistent with the direction of change in the social frame.

This adds two additional nuances to the analysis offered in chapter 4 regarding the conditions for successful cooperation. First, goal formation is fundamental in choosing between the strategies of cooperation and defection under conditions of social dilemma. Realism has tended to narrowly emphasize the corrosive effect of relative gains on cooperation, and it has largely ignored the possibility that states might also seek cooperation as an attempt to improve their comparative position or prevent relative decline. Liberals also hold that relative gains seeking can only damage existing cooperation and sour the prospects for new agreements.

Under prospect theory, risk acceptance can lead governments to accept new forms of cooperation even when this represents a risky strategy with an expected outcome of further loss. This holds regardless of the goals that governments seek, that is, whether the goal is enrichment or an improved comparative position. However, as both risk acceptance and relative gains sensitivity coincide with a losses frame, prospect theory suggests that governments often seek cooperation as a relative gains strategy. Contrary to both realism and liberalism, it is therefore possible for governments to be sensitive to relative position and still energetically pursue cooperative strategies. Such cooperation represents an attempt to secure relative gains that are impossible to achieve unilaterally. This constitutes a new and therefore understudied argument about the motivations for cooperation.

Second, sensitivity to relative gains often transforms the matrix of incentives in social dilemmas (e.g., Stein 1990). Given the preference structure a>b>c>d, figure 5.1 defines a traditional PD game. Under conditions of loss, however, governments will be acutely sensitive to changes in relative position. Rival accomplishments now contain negative externalities for both sides, such that the importance of differences between returns dominates individualistic assessments of one's own payoffs. This alters the preference order. While both retain defection as the dominant strategy, the concern for relative gains produces the transformed matrix given in figure 5.2. Under a traditional PD, the equilibrium outcome in the lower right cell is Pareto deficient. Both states would be better off under mutual cooperation. Under a losses frame and relative gains seeking, this is no longer the case.

Thus, under conditions of loss, maintaining cooperation in established relationships will be difficult even with robust institutions place. Chapter 4 initially described why risk acceptance alone makes this so. The relative gains seeking that accompanies a losses frames reinforces this pattern. Additionally, in a matrix transformed by sensitivity to relative gains, the underlying attractiveness of mutual cooperation diminishes. Earlier predictions about strategy, and the current discussion of goal formation, are therefore consistent and reinforcing. Existing cooperative relationships are fundamentally undermined by losses frames, as are the traditional conceptions about the promotive functions of international institutions. In contrast, under a gains frame changes in relative position will have little effect, contrary to the predictions of realism. Relative decline, if it results from mutual absolute gains, promotes risk aversion and a traditional interpretation of PD incentives. Here, governments focus upon their own payoffs, and the functions ascribed to regimes by liberals—reducing transactions costs, monitoring compliance, and so forth—are much more likely to be effective in sustaining cooperation.

		State A	
		Cooperate	Defect
State B	Cooperate	b, b	d, a
	Defect	a, d	c, c

FIGURE 5.1. Generic prisoner's dilemma
Assuming a preference order of a>b>c>d, with governments
insensitive to changes in relative position.

		State A	
		Cooperate	Defect
State B	Cooperate	b or c, c or b	d, a
	Defect	a, d	c or b, b or c

FIGURE 5.2. Prisoner's dilemma transformed by relative gains
Assuming a preference order of a>b>c>d, with governments very
sensitive to changes in relative position.

CONCLUSION

In its purest form, realism asserts that "the fundamental goal of states in any relationship is to prevent others from achieving advances in their relative capabilities" (Grieco 1988, 498). Liberalism counters that "the existence of international regimes composed of sovereign entities that voluntarily eschew independent decision making" is evidence of a world in which states maximize absolute gains (Stein 1983, 134). The purpose of this chapter has been to sketch the contours of an alternative set of theorems for state goals grounded in prospect theory.

The next two chapters attempt a preliminary empirical evaluation of several of the hypotheses developed up to this point through an examination of the Montreal Protocol. Rather than focusing exclusively upon a single implication of prospect theory, as previous studies have done, several of the ideas developed here will be examined simultaneously. While more challenging empirically, this approach permits a detailed evaluation of prospect theory's potential to both generate meaningful theories of international relations and develop an integrated set of empirically supported propositions of the kind offered by rational choice.

The analysis will focus upon the behavior of the European Community (EC) and the United States during the Montreal Protocol negotiations that were initiated to limit the release of ozone destroying chlorofluorocarbons (CFCs) into the atmosphere. It is not possible to examine all of the propositions outlined here. Still, the Montreal Protocol does provide an opportunity to explore several of the implications of prospect theory for the study of international politics, including the conditions for successful cooperation, the unintended consequences of power, risk assessment, and gains preference.

In the EC case, the central empirical puzzle is explaining a midstream shift from absolute to relative gains pursuit. Before the onset of negotiations, the EC experienced both relative and absolute gains in CFC production and trade. Realism predicts that EC policy during the negotiations would attempt to protect recent relative gains in the international CFC trade and solidify its newfound position as the dominant international supplier to the global market. Liberalism, by contrast, predicts protection of recently increased production levels. At minimum, we would expect a consistent policy when the EC is forced to choose between relative and absolute gains. However, EC policy was not consistent, and on this point alone the traditional division between realist and liberal theory is challenged. By contrast, the behavior of the EC is consistent with the new framework offered here.

The discussion of the U.S. case begins by focusing upon the early attempts to secure an international agreement, which initially languished under a reluctant international community. This reluctance included the United States, which did little to press for a treaty. However, American policymakers did eventually become strong advocates. In fact, American leadership was ultimately crucial in securing an international agreement. While other studies have explored the events that led to the Montreal Protocol, this American about-face has received surprisingly little attention. The American break to multilateralism was prompted by the creation of a losses frame that in turn motivated a risk-acceptant strategy to push for an international agreement.

This losses frame was constructed for policymakers as a by-product of CFC industry lobbying efforts to forestall domestic and international regulation.

The EC and the U.S. cases reveal important differences in the processes by which decision frames are constituted. For the EC, a decision frame was created by changes in the international political topography that were largely beyond its control. For the United States, changes in the domestic political discourse led to the construction of a frame. Combined, the U.S. and EC cases suggest that the set of contextual and structural arrangements in which states are motivated to action are not just objective. Rather, if we are to connect context to action, context is best understood from the government's point of view.

Finally, testing realist and liberal propositions against the behavior of states operating in the domain of environmental politics would seem to bias against realism. Traditionally, realist claims are limited to so-called high politics, and the common assumption has been that liberal analysis is perhaps the better framework with which to examine issues like environmental treaty making that do not impinge directly upon security. However, modern realism also claims an explanatory advantage in low politics. Grieco, for example, asserts that "realism is superior to neoliberalism in explaining important political-economic events," and that this is true even when the governments involved are close allies (1990, 12, 13). There are as well a number of studies that demonstrate that relative gains seeking affects cooperation in low politics (e.g., Mastanduno 1991; Haskel 1974), and evidence that average citizens are often concerned with relative gains in the domain of low politics (Herman, Tetlock, and Diascro 2001). All of this suggests that realist insights about relative position ought to be taken seriously in even those empirical domains that are normally considered to lie under the purview of liberalism.

Chapter 6

The European Community

Previous chapters developed a set of arguments about state behavior derived from prospect theory. This chapter and the next examine some of these predictions against the behavior of states participant to the Montreal Protocol. The focus of these two chapters is not treaty specifics, but instead the evolving positions of the European Community (EC) and United States during the negotiations.

Background

European Community participation in the negotiations can be separated into two stages. The first began in the early 1980s and concluded with the Vienna Convention, which did little to protect the ozone layer but called for further talks. The second stage began shortly after the signing of the Vienna Convention in 1985 and concluded in 1987 at Montreal with a binding protocol. Prior to the negotiations, the EC enjoyed both relative and absolute gains in the production and sale of CFCs. Realism predicts that the EC would protect recent relative gains in the international CFC trade and solidify its newfound position as the dominant international supplier to the global market, and that this would make securing an agreement difficult or impossible. Liberalism predicts protection of recently increased production levels. These are not necessarily exclusive goals; however, the EC was not able to pursue them simultaneously.[1] We would expect, therefore, a consistent policy from the EC—that it would choose either absolute gains or relative position. In fact, EC policy was not consistent and shifted from protection of production levels to the pursuit of relative gains.

Prospect theory explains such changes in policy by context. The discussion that follows establishes first that the decision frame for the EC switched from gains to losses in the period between Vienna and Montreal. With this change in the decision frame, EC policy went from absolute gains pursuit and risk avoidance to relative gains pursuit and risk acceptance. That is, under a gains frame, EC behavior is consistent with liberalism. Under a losses frame, the EC abandoned absolute gains and, consistent with realism, chased relative position. Additionally, it was not until the onset of a losses frame that the EC gambled on a negotiated settlement as part of a strategy to secure advantages in relative position through cooperation.

FOREIGN POLICY IN A COMMUNITY

An initial objection to applying theories of state behavior to the EC is that this artificially constructs the EC as a single negotiating entity when, in fact, important differences exist among member states. However, a combination of domestic politics, internal EC power relations, and EC decision-making procedures makes this construction both historically accurate and theoretically useful.[2]

In the EC legislature, the Commission of the European Communities develops and proposes legislation to the Council of Ministers for ratification. Before the council adopts legislation, it usually elicits an opinion from the Parliament, which is composed of representatives from each member state. While the participation of the Parliament allows for public input into the process of policy formation, much of the final form of EC policy is fashioned behind closed doors in the council. Indeed, EC policy is formulated "largely in secret—following the traditions of diplomacy—and legislation is adopted by a Council of Ministers behind closed doors," so that "it is still possible for EC legislation to differ in significant respects from the proposal originally published by the commission without outsiders knowing who was responsible for the changes or why" (Haigh 1991, 167).

The authority of the EC to negotiate binding treaties with other countries evolved gradually through a series of European Court of Justice rulings. Where the EC has "competence," the commission is charged to negotiate on behalf of the EC in accordance with a council mandate that must be unanimously approved. The commission has continually attempted to expand its authority by claiming competence to negotiate new issues while the council, composed of national ministers, is often more protective of member state interests.[3] Prior to the Single European Act, which gave the EC competence in environmental affairs, it was not clear that the commission had authority to negotiate a CFC ban on behalf of the EC. However, because CFC regulations would directly impact the relations of production across member states, a uniform EC policy was mandated (Jachtenfuchs 1990, 262). The commission was accordingly given authority by the council to enter into negotiations under a unanimously approved council mandate.

Still, the commission was less than secure in its jurisdiction and was unwilling to antagonize the council by demanding a negotiating mandate that would permit sufficient latitude to negotiate a compromise agreement. Rather, the commission's concern was with establishing a solid precedent for competence in international environmental treaty making, and it was therefore willing to sacrifice effectiveness for authority. This initially crippled the negotiations because the commission, "negotiating on behalf of the Community, was thus condemned to immobility without being able to react to compromise proposals" (Benedick 1991, 70). Indeed, that the commission's primary concern was establishing competence was clear even to external groups such as the European Environmental Bureau, which maintained that the commission was concerned more with the internal balance of power within the EC than in securing an effective international treaty (Jachtenfuchs 1990, 264).

Furthermore, under unanimous decisions rules, any single member possesses a veto over group decisions. In the context of the Montreal Protocol negotiations, this meant that "[s]tates strongly influenced by their respective chemical industries could force others [in the community] to join their position. This meant harmonization at the lowest common denominator. In the last resort, it was the successful lobbying of two chemical companies at the national, and not at the European level which determined the international position of the Community" (Jachtenfuchs 1990, 275).

Britain and France, on behalf of domestic chemical producers (most notably France's Atochem and Britain's Imperial Chemical Industries), were able to dominate early EC policies and negotiating positions. Initially, industry representatives frequently served as official state delegates. The shared perception was that "industry representatives substituted themselves [for] politicians in the decision making" process within the EC (Faucheux and Noel 1988, 24). In addition, the council negotiating mandate given to the commission was extremely restrictive, allowing no room for real negotiation, and did not realistically address the threat of ozone depletion.[4]

A more flexible council mandate might have mitigated the influence of the British and French delegations. Absent this, and given the weak position of the commission and a unanimous decision rule, for practical purposes and throughout most of the negotiations, there was in fact a single EC position that closely paralleled the interests of the large CFC producing states, Britain and France.[5]

THE DECISION FRAME PRIOR TO VIENNA

During the interval between the U.S. unilateral ban on aerosols in 1978 and the negotiations resulting in the Vienna Convention, CFC-producing states in the EC enjoyed significant gains. The U.S. reaction to the initial ozone depletion thesis (promulgated in 1974) was to ban CFC aerosol propellants for nonessential uses by 1978. The result was a 95 percent decrease in U.S. production of CFCs for aerosols, and this allowed EC producers to capture both relative and absolute gains in the global sale of highly profitable CFCs. Eventually, the EC overtook the United States as the world's largest producer.[6] The EC had also become the single largest producer of CFCs for export and was the only remaining significant supplier of CFCs to global markets. By 1985, EC exports had risen 43 percent over 1976 levels and accounted for fully 30 percent of total EC production (CEC 1985). CFCs also grew to become more important to the aggregate EC economy, accounting for 50 percent more of GNP in the EC than they did in the United States (Congress 1988).

The forecast for growth in global CFC demand was also promising. Many developing nations were just entering a period of economic expansion that would increasingly require CFCs for domestic products. These included, by order of potential use, China, India, Brazil, Saudi Arabia, South Korea, Indonesia, Nigeria, Mexico, Turkey, and Argentina (Haaga 1987). For example, China, India, and Brazil were projected to have annual growth rates in consumption of 12 percent, 15 percent, and 8 percent, respectively, from a 1986 baseline (Munasinghe and King 1991, 9). Developing countries were also increasing imports of goods that required CFCs for their manufacture. The increase in demand represented an important potential market for EC producers. In 1986, EC production capacity was about 30 to 40 percent above actual production levels. When combined with its exclusive position as the world's supplier, this excess capacity meant that EC producers were uniquely positioned to capitalize efficiently on emerging CFC markets.

Moreover, the perception within the EC was that it had responded adequately to the ozone threat and that no further actions were required. After its ban on aerosols, the United States initiated bilateral discussions intended to compel the EC to enact similar restrictions. The EC responded in 1980 with a proposal for reducing CFC aerosol use by 30 percent from 1976 levels by 1982. This was largely a symbolic concession intended to placate U.S. demands for action as that level of reductions Ahad already been reached at the time the decision was taken" (Jachtenfuchs 1990, 213). However, the proposal allowed the EC to claim that it was not blind to the ozone issue and had taken measures commensurate with the current level of scientific understanding.[7] Thus, decision makers in the EC had dealt with the ozone issue in such a way as not to harm its status as the dominant exporter or its positioning to capitalize on future growth in international demand.

It is this set of preconvention conditions which constitutes the reference point from which EC negotiating positions derived. In the initial period leading up to the 1985 Vienna Convention, the recent gains by CFC producers in the EC were impressive. Better still, if developing-country growth estimates proved correct, market demand was expected to increase dramatically. The diplomatic history that follows will in part demonstrate that throughout the negotiations, it is an evaluation of the status quo relative to this reference point that drives EC negotiation strategies.

NEGOTIATING AT VIENNA: 1982–1985

Despite important unanswered scientific questions about the precise nature of the link between of CFCs and ozone depletion, the issue of ozone protection nonetheless gained wide international acceptance. In 1981, the United Nations Environmental Program (UNEP) placed the issue atop its agenda and by 1982 talks to negotiate a binding protocol began in Vienna.

By 1984, the U.S. position, along with the other members of the so-called Toronto Group, was that a global ban on the nonessential use of CFC aerosol propellants was the quickest way to address ozone depletion. U.S. experience with such a ban suggested that this approach produced limited negative economic consequences. In contrast, EC representatives downplayed the need for a treaty. They argued that the scientific evidence on ozone depletion was incomplete, that no effective substitutes existed or would exist soon, and that hasty action based on questionable science would be costly.[8] U.S. delegates decried the EC position, attributing it to the influence of CFC producers whose aim seemed to be "to avoid for as long as possible the costs of switching to alternative products" (Benedick 1991, 33).

The inevitable clash between the Toronto Group and EC positions eventually deadlocked the negotiations. The EC stubbornly stuck to its initial proposal. Without compromise, it quickly became clear to all that no binding agreement was possible at Vienna by the 1985 deadline. The negotiations then devolved into a discussion of side issues, including an attempt to get a nonbinding convention that would include a statement on the need for increased research into the mechanisms of ozone depletion and, if possible, further talks to conclude subsequently in Montreal.

RELATIVE OR ABSOLUTE GAINS?

From the perspective of realism, this EC intransigence is a bit difficult to grasp. If, as realism asserts, governments are primarily motivated by relative gains, then the Vienna stalemate represents a missed opportunity for EC negotiators. EC representatives did offer a proposal consisting largely of a 30 percent reduction in the domestic use of CFCs in aerosols from a 1976 base-line—levels at which Europe was already operating (Lammers 1988). EC delegates did not, however, pursue a production capacity cap as an alternative. A capacity freeze clearly favored those counties with excess production capacity by locking out other countries which did not yet produce CFCs or were already operating at full capacity. This included many large developing countries and the United States. By contrast, EC facilities were producing at about 65 percent of their maximum capacity. With the projected growth in global demand, such a cap would allow the EC to continue its increasing share in global markets as EC producers would remain the single supplier able to meet increasing international demand, thereby locking in Europe's position as the dominant supplier to the global market. Estimates suggested that EC producers could continue to unilaterally increases production for perhaps two decades[9] and, with a capacity cap, potential competitors would be prevented from challenging the dominant position of EC producers.

Realism therefore predicts a more aggressive EC counterproposal in which the EC offers to accept some meaningful cuts in aerosol use in exchange for a global production capacity freeze. A reduction of CFCs as aerosol propellants would imply a loss, in absolute terms, for domestic producers of CFCs. However, the U.S. experience with such a ban demonstrated that the effect on the overall economy was minimal at worst. Substitute propellants proved inexpensive and safe, and the increased cost to the consumer of switching to safe alternatives was negligible.[10] Available data also suggested that the short-term loss to the EC in absolute terms, even if it had to eliminate CFCs as aerosol propellants altogether, would be small.[11] However, the potential relative gains possible under a capacity cap were significant. A cap would secure an even more favorable distribution of production in a growing market while effectively preventing newcomers from entering. Realism thus predicts that EC policy makers would be willing to compromise on the U.S. demand for an aerosol ban in exchange for a capacity cap. Instead, however, EC decision makers deliberately undermined the attempt to get a binding protocol by adopting the position that any cuts to current usage levels would be unacceptable.

Participants in the negotiations seemed bemused by the EC's position. U.S. ambassador Richard Benedick attributed the EC's early intransigence to cultural differences. To make the point, he quoted French philosopher Alexis de Tocqueville: "I do not think, on the whole, that there is more selfishness among us (Europeans) than in America; the only difference is that there it is enlightened, here it is not. Each American knows when to sacrifice some of his private interests to save the rest; we want to save everything, and often we lose it all" (Benedick 1991, 30).[12]

However, the EC position was not simply a case of wrong-headed negotiating. The restrictive negotiating mandate passed down from the council was deliberately designed to shackle the commission, preventing it from negotiating in any meaningful sense of the term. As one observer noted, "For its part consistent with its 'status quo' decision, the EC Commission declared that it had no mandate to negotiate anything other than a cap on production capacity. EC and UK representatives then attempted to postpone the next round from the previously scheduled February 1987 date until April. . . . When the plenary rejected this tactic, the heads of the UK and EC Commission delegations departed from Geneva prematurely" (Benedick 1991, 70). This represents a strategy designed to opt out of the negotiations altogether. The clear signal was that Europe was not prepared nor willing to negotiate on any form of restrictions in CFC use, as the council mandate under which EC representatives operated "left no room for CFC reductions in the Vienna discussions" (Jachtenfuchs 1990, 263).[13]

While realism cannot predict the EC decision to opt out of negotiation, forgo an attempt to capitalize on relative gains, and thereby solidify its position over the United States, this decision is predicted by prospect theory. As demonstrated earlier, the decision to commit to negotiation constitutes a gamble in which the outcome is unknown. In addition, given recent gains in production, an improved market position, and the projections of continued increased demand, the EC was clearly operating under a gains frame. When confronted with the choice between the beneficial status quo that required nothing more than intransigence and a gamble for increased relative gains that required entering into negotiations in good faith, prospect theory predicts that the EC would forgo an opportunity to improve its relative position in favor of the status quo. States will not actively pursue relative position in a gains frame, as realism predicts, if in such pursuit they must risk existing benefits.

This is true even when the potential costs of negotiating are likely to be small relative to the potential benefits. U.S. experience with the aerosol ban demonstrated that the costs were minimal, while the potential relative gains of a capacity cap were large. But under a gains frame the EC was not pursuing relative position. Instead, EC strategy served to protect current absolute levels of production. Remaining immobile and effectively opting out of the negotiations shielded CFC producers against American attempts to curtail the absolute gains in production achieved following unilateral U.S. restrictions. Befuddling from a realist standpoint, the EC position becomes clear under the perspective developed here. The refusal to negotiate reflected the EC desire to avoid the risk inherent in engaging in meaningful negotiations and protect absolute gains. Both goals are consistent with the description of states as prudent maximizers operating under a gains frame.

An agreement including a capacity cap was a real possibility. While such a proposal would have clearly favored EC interests, the United States never argued against a capacity cap, even though it would lock domestic producers out of international markets. The United States was operating at capacity so the decision to compete for a greater international market share would necessarily be an expensive one anyway. In addition, while disagreement existed over the exact levels at which capacity should be capped, all participants recognized that the cap had the distinct advantage of placing a lid on other nonaerosol uses of CFCs (Lammers 1988). Such uses comprised the fastest growing sector of the CFC market, so an EC proposal could have honestly claimed to be more comprehensive. Finally, throughout the Vienna negotiations, the only consistent U.S. demand was for an aerosol ban.[14] This is not to suggest that the EC necessarily would have been successful. The point here is that such a proposal was not attempted. EC behavior is therefore inconsistent with the realist prediction that states continually strive for relative gains.

Now, it is also possible to interpret the EC strategy at Viennia as simply consistent with liberalism. Indeed, the above discussion establishes the EC as protective of absolute gains. However, EC policy changed after Vienna. With a shift in the decision frame from gains to losses, the community quickly abandoned its defense of current production levels while becoming an active participant in the negotiations in order to chase relative position.

THE FORMATION OF A LOSSES FRAME

While the Vienna talks did not result in a binding protocol, the participants did continue discussions. After a brief respite, they agreed to attempt a treaty in Montreal by late 1987. It was during this hiatus—immediately following Vienna and prior to Montreal—that several aspects of the political topography changed, altering the implications of the status quo for the EC. The changes included threatened U.S. trade legislation, an emerging scientific consensus on the link of CFCs to ozone depletion, and a reversal in the position of American producers of CFCs on the desirability of a binding protocol.

U.S. Unilateral Action

In May of 1986, the Natural Resources Defense Council (NRDC) sued the Environmental Protection Agency (EPA) under section 157(b) of the Clean Air Act. The section requires the EPA to issue "regulations for the control of any substance, practice, process or activity . . . [that] may reasonably be anticipated to affect the stratosphere, especially the ozone in the stratosphere."[15]

The suit alleged that the EPA was not carrying out its duties under the act. The district court agreed and ordered the EPA to publish a set of proposed regulations by May 1, 1987, and to submit final regulations for CFC restrictions later that year.

Consequently, the United States was again moving to restrict CFC emissions unilaterally. This initially seemed a repeat of earlier US action on aerosols that benefitted EC producers. U.S. industry would have to integrate more expensive substitutes into manufacturing processes, and domestic producers had cultivated few clients outside the United States to which they could send the surplus production that would result from a decline in domestic consumption. This time, however, concerns about international competitiveness also produced a spate of congressional attempts to manipulate the negotiations in Montreal.[16] The introduction of ozone protection bills reflected a concern by Congress that international negotiations might ultimately fail at the very moment that the U.S. would be required to unilaterally restrict CFC use.

Some in Congress appeared to be primarily concerned about adverse environmental consequences and were upset that the EPA had to be sued in order to carry out its mandate. This view played out in open session. Congressman Waxman's lashing of EPA chief Lee Thomas was typical: "My question to you is, while we all want an international agreement, are we willing to accept the 24 percent level increase in the United States? Are we willing to accept a 40 percent increase, or is there some level of increase that we're going to say is not going to be tolerable in this country, while we're waiting for an international agreement?" (U.S. Congress, 1987a, 137).

At the same hearing, Congressman Bates asks, "Is the Environmental Protection Agency's primary value or goal to preserve the health and protect life or is it to protect the profit and the jobs and the associated costs? And I recognize that those are valid considerations that should be debated, but I don't think that the goal of the Environmental Protection Agency is to weigh those considerations" (U.S. Congress 1987a, 115).

Still, this congressional concern for the ozone layer manifests itself only after the NRDC suit, and even then only as the court-ordered deadline for new regulations approached. The actual target of trade legislation was not the EPA, but a reluctant international community. Distressed at the slow pace of the negotiations, Congress attempted to force the issue and also ensure that the United States would not be disadvantaged if the talks failed. For example, the author of the Stratospheric Ozone and Climate Protection Act declared, "[M]y preference is still that this global problem be dealt with by way of international agreement," and then threatened, "[C]all it what you will, countries that wish to trade with us will have to abide by our rules for protecting the environment" (*Cong. Rec.* 1987). Each of the proposed bills attempted to create incentives designed to limit the possibility of European producer free riding.

In addition to a unilateral phaseout of CFCs and restrictions on imports in bulk, these bills all proposed in some way to halt the import of all goods that used CFCs in their manufacture.[17]

To make the intent of the proposed domestic legislation clear, the U.S. delegation to the negotiations took care to draw attention to these domestic efforts. Delegates went so far as to suggest that the domestic forces that desired strong action were beyond control and, if no effective multilateral pact was signed, domestic legislation was inevitable (Benedick 1987). U.S. representatives also Amade certain that the implications of this threat were not lost on foreign governments, pointing out that there might be a price to pay for not joining in meaningful efforts to protect the ozone layer" (Benedick 1991, 29). In his opening plenary comments at Vienna, the head of the U.S. delegation highlighted EC intransigence and placed attention upon congressional efforts. Noting that "people are beginning to say that some parties to these negotiations seem to be viewing the ozone issue mainly in terms of narrow self-interest," he then threatened, "[D]istinguished delegates, I cannot emphasize too strongly the high degree of interest in the United Sates in the outcome of these negotiations. . . . Last week, a bipartisan coalition introduced a concurrent resolution" intending to eliminate the use of CFCs in the United States and "stop making them and refuse to import them" (Benedick 1987, 14).

The impact of these legislative threats went far to change the implications of the status quo for the EC. If international talks failed, the United States would act unilaterally. Importantly, EC members that were not major producers also found themselves targeted in the proposed legislation. These governments now had a stake in the outcome of the negotiations and no longer remained disinterested parties willing to defer to producing states. The tactic was effective. The reaction of nonproducing governments demonstrated that "even mere talk" of trade restrictions got the acute attention of EC government officials. (Wirth 1987, 258). Producing states also took U.S. threats seriously. In what was a typical refrain, a French delegate noted that the American position was initially discounted, but that "we did not realize that the U.S. took it [ozone depletion] seriously. Now we do" (U.S. Congress 1987a).

While important, it would be a mistake to overestimate the influence of this single factor. A comprehensive ban of products that require CFCs in their manufacture would be expensive. The value of such products was far greater than the receipts from production of CFCs in bulk. Also, some in Congress, consistent with their long-standing support of free trade policies, were unwilling to impose market closure for ozone protection, or to accept the significant costs associated with likely retaliatory EC trade legislation. Finally, members of Congress often introduce bills only for constituent consumption; such bills are never intended to become law. Still, the United States did signal to the international community that there was no domestic support for the position that the United States should bear the full burden of environmental protection unilaterally, and therefore that some trade restrictions were likely if the talks failed to produce an agreement.

Scientific Consensus

A primary component of the EC's blocking strategy at Vienna was to argue that the science of ozone depletion was at best inconclusive. While EC governments declared their concern about the possibility of ozone depletion, given current science, a guarded response was all that could be justified. In fact, the EC was initially correct in asserting that there was not yet any conclusive empirical evidence linking CFCs to ozone depletion, nor conclusive evidence of depletion itself, and that there was significant disagreement within the scientific community as to the nature of the relationship between ozone, CFCs, and atmospheric dynamics.[18] This changed, however, and by 1987 the scientific community formed a consensus on the nature of the link between CFCs and ozone depletion.

While it fell short of a binding protocol, the Vienna Convention did establish a mechanism for international cooperation and coordination of ozone research. If the ozone layer was threatened, this cooperation was supposed to provide the institutional infrastructure necessary to produce consensus on the impact of CFCs. National scientists had been working independently, but they now shared resources and data and could quickly verify suggestive findings. The conclusions of independent studies quickly converged and "progressively delimited the range of possible disagreements that could credibly be attributed to different views of science" (Parson 1992, 28).

A NASA-coordinated study, published in July 1986, settled the scientific case against CFCs. Because the report had garnered broad international financial support, its conclusions carried significant political weight (Hass 1992, 35).[19] Atmospheric scientists concluded that the threat to the ozone was authentic, and that CFCs deserved attention as the major culprit. The study also noted that CFC molecules were potentially several thousand times more potent than carbon dioxide as a greenhouse gas. These conclusions motivated a series of UNEP and EPA workshops. Under the newfound institutional cooperation, predictions from the newest atmospheric models were quickly compiled and disseminated. A general consensus formed around the notion that ozone depletion would continue even under a freeze of CFC emissions at current levels.[20]

It is important to stress that, at this point (1986–1987), there still existed no hard empirical evidence outside the laboratory to support the ozone depletion hypothesis. The various scenarios for depletion rates were derived from elaborate computer simulations. Competing models incorporated different assumptions about the rate of CFC emissions, the transfer rate into the stratosphere, atmospheric dynamics, and the impact of other trace chemicals.[21] Nonetheless, while the models differed somewhat in their predictions, there emerged a consensus around the notion of depletion itself. There was also a rough convergence in the predicted rate of depletion given current rates of CFC consumption.

The political impact was immediate. During a protocol workshop in Leesberg, Virginia, all participants except for the EC agreed on the need to act. If current estimates proved correct, some form of international regime would be the only effective method to halt the depletion of the ozone layer.[22] This consensus also increased the probability of U.S. unilateral action should international efforts fail. Lee Thomas, whose EPA was under court order to implement CFC regulations in the United States, was now convinced that "considerable evidence exists, both in theory and from models, linking these chemicals to depletion of ozone" (U.S. Department of State 1986, 1). Operating under a federal court order to issue domestic regulations consistent with his agency's assessment of the degree of the threat, Thomas's judgment was of crucial interest to both U.S. and EC policymakers because unilateral EPA action to restrict CFC use would increase the probability of congressional trade legislation.

Thus, the emergence of a scientific consensus was part of the shift in the status quo for the EC. While a strong international protocol was by no means certain, the perception that the EC would be operating under some form of CFC regime or U.S. trade strictures considerably increased.

Industry Shift

Shortly after the initial U.S. aerosol ban, domestic CFC producers formed the Alliance for Responsible CFC Policy, and were very successful in opposing additional attempts to restrict CFC production and use. Suddenly, U.S. domestic producers broke ranks with their European counterparts and came out in support of an international agreement. Because they could not see any other rational reason for this shift, EC delegates deeply "distrusted the motives behind the U.S. position" and suspected any strong regulatory proposal coming from the United States could only mean that American industry had secretly developed CFC substitutes (Litfin 1992, 267). Further proof of a conspiracy was found in the fact that the push for regulations seemingly counter to industrial interests was coming from a Republican administration whose antiregulation credentials were unquestioned.

There was in fact no secret plan to flood the market with substitutes, but this about-face did add to the EC's troubles. The public explanation for the alliance's flip on the issue was that the science of ozone depletion was compelling enough to justify some limited international action. Alliance head Richard Barnett noted that "in fact, all of the computer models calculate that large future growth in CFC emissions may contribute to significant ozone depletion in the latter half of the next century" (Barnett 1987, 342). That an industry with a seemingly clear interest in preventing restrictions joined the call for international action seriously undercut the EC's position.

The about-face by U.S. producers "broke industry's transatlantic united front on the eve of the negotiations, [and was] greeted with consternation in Europe" (Benedick 1991, 32). More importantly, it permitted U.S. negotiators to claim that they had domestic industry in agreement on the need for international regulations. While this overstated industry's actual support, it did demonstrate a weakening of domestic opposition to an international agreement.[23] Even those in Congress who argued for unilateral trade legislation, some as an incentive for the EC to negotiate seriously, claimed industry support.[24] Thus, the U.S. negotiating position was significantly strengthened, as was the perception that the domestic political context was now much more open to regulation.

Alone, any one of these three factors was not likely to have changed the EC's assessment of the status quo. For example, the EC had fended off earlier U.S. bilateral attempts to secure a ban of CFC aerosol propellants. Together, however, they represented a significant shift in the prevailing political winds and constituted a viable challenge to the status quo in the form of multilateral action without the EC as participant, U.S. unilateral action, or both. If current conditions continued along this trajectory, when evaluated against a pre-Vienna Convention reference point, the status quo now carried the possibility of significant losses for the EC in the forms outlined above. Prospect theory suggests that this new evaluation of the status quo will produce risk acceptance. Such a change in strategy manifests quickly. For the first time, the EC committed meaningfully to negotiation and, in so doing, abandoned its concern for absolute gains while protecting its relative position in the CFC trade.

THE EUROPEAN GAMBLE

In late 1986, the European Commission reassessed the most recent scientific conclusions regarding CFCs, the cost and effectiveness of alternative control schemes, and the status of the international negotiations. It submitted a report to the council along with a request for a revised negotiating mandate. While the report noted the aforementioned NASA study and the consensus that emerged in meetings thereafter, the commission nonetheless concluded that "the present Community measures for controlling the use and in particular the production of CFCs represent an intrinsically sound framework" and that "the Commission considers that the status quo in respect of the existing Council Decisions on CFCs in the environment should be maintained" (CEC 1986, 9). Despite this reaffirmation, the commission also deftly presented the council with an opportunity to alter the EC's posture at the next round of negotiations. Lauding past EC actions to protect the ozone, the commission cautiously suggested that "modification in detail may be required in the context of a regulatory system" (CEC 1986, 9). The strategy was a sensible one. Intended to minimize the risk inherent in entering into serious negotiations, a more relaxed interpretation permitted the commission to negotiate minor issues like timetables for implementation and verification procedures, but it did not allow the commission to move substantially away from the existing community position.

The strategy also contained considerable risk. Continued EC intransigence was the single significant remaining barrier to a new international CFC regime, and meaningful participation in the negotiations would give further momentum to its establishment. The result could run counter to EC interests, especially given both the regulatory momentum apparent in the United States and the emerging scientific consensus. Indeed, now committed to negotiations, it quickly became clear that a more realistic posture was required. The scientific consensus linking CFCs to ozone depletion, when combined with new findings that the rate of CFC emissions had drastically increased in the 1980s, allowed proponents of a protocol to argue that, at the very least, a freeze on current emissions was needed while more conclusive studies were conducted. To participate meaningfully and have its proposals taken seriously, the EC abandoned its position on absolute gains. Dropped entirely was its defense of CFCs as aerosol propellants. What in previous rounds had been nonnegotiable was now no longer even a point of discussion. Under a looser council mandate, and during meetings in early 1987, the commission offered that it would be willing to discuss the impact (economic and ecological) of a production freeze, but that this was not an official negotiating position. This move constituted "an important concession," and the negotiations were now fully engaged for the first time (Lammers 1988, 237).[25]

Having abandoned protection of absolute gains, the EC turned attention to its relative position in the export markets. This defense of relative position is most clearly evidenced in the contentious debate surrounding attempts to develop an accounting scheme for achieving a freeze or, if agreed to, reductions.

The contrasting accounting formulas for measuring CFC emissions proposed by the EC and the United States affected states differently depending upon their level of exports. The United States proposed an "adjusted production" approach, while the EC offered a simple production freeze. Either scheme would bring the United States and the EC to about the same absolute levels of CFC production. However, under the adjusted production approach, the EC would have to halt exports in order to avoid heavier cuts.[26] At issue here was the relative position of the EC as the major exporter to the international market. The main consequences of the adjusted production promoted by the United States would be to equalize production and export levels between the community and the United States. A simple production freeze would not require the EC to give up its position as the dominant international supplier. For this reason, the EC vigorously rejected the American proposal (Lammers 1988, 251).

This defense of relative position demonstrates EC priorities once it committed to negotiations. As prospect theory predicts, under a losses frame, the EC abandoned its protection of status quo production levels and attempted instead to maintain a relative position as the major exporter to global markets. In addition, unlike when it was operating in a gains frame, the EC was now risk acceptant and attempted to use the negotiations to secure relative gains. Committing to a settlement which, given the U.S. position, might require cuts in production represented a gamble as part of a strategy to protect its international position. Indeed, to the extent that an effective protocol required active community participation, it is the risk acceptance of the EC that in the end permitted a successful agreement.

CONCLUSION

This second round of negotiations found conclusion in the Montreal Protocol that achieved a rough compromise between the U.S. defense of a total production ban and the EC position of the status quo. It is important to note that there was little scientific justification for the levels of production allowed under the protocol. The best scientific conclusions called for significantly greater reductions. This, combined with the understanding that no empirical evidence outside the laboratory directly connected CFCs to ozone depletion, suggests that science was not the only or even primary reason for the protocol. While science played an important role, those looking to the international community's reaction to ozone science as a model to resolve other international environmental commons dilemmas—most notably global warming—should recognize that the final agreement in Montreal was a political compromise. It was not until shortly after the signing of the Montreal Protocol that the scientific community uncovered the first empirical evidence outside the laboratory linking CFCs to the ozone hole over Antarctica. A provision in the protocol allowed for periodic review if the understanding of the problem changed dramatically. With this incontrovertible evidence of damage to the earth's protective shield, the global community acted responsibly, and the protocol was amended to eliminate virtually all CFC and Halon use in signatory countries.

It might also be inferred from the above that the EC's partial acquiescence resulted primarily from the threatened exercise of American power within the issue area. Congressional threats were explicit. However, as noted here, it is not certain that the United States would have acted, and the EC had fought off a previous American bilateral attempt to secure concessions. Rather, the evidence suggests that threatened U.S. trade legislation was one of a number of changes in the political topography which together solidified a losses frame for the EC. More importantly, even if we were to grant a traditional power explanation as a reason for the EC's decision to negotiate, it cannot account for the shift in EC policy from absolute to relative gains pursuit. There is no conventional logic connecting such an application of power to a shift from absolute to relative gains policy. There is also no evidence that the United States desired such a shift in EC preferences. That the EC both risked negotiations and changed to relative gains pursuit only after the onset of a losses frame suggests strong evidence for prospect theory.

Nonetheless, power is not unimportant for this analysis. Chapters 3 and 5 suggested that one possible unintended consequence of power is that it may alter the decision frame of the target. Here, to the extent that power helped create a losses frame, it is part of the explanation for the change in EC preferences and policy. Rather than a direct link between U.S. threats and EC actions, prospect theory suggests that the link is indirect. Because the decision to enter into negotiations is a gamble, and because states in the losses frame exhibit greater risk acceptance and pursue relative gains, the link connecting U.S. power and EC choices is the constitution of a losses frame. Finally, contemporary realist arguments about the corrosive effect of sensitivity to relative position on attempts to secure cooperation are modified by this analysis. Because under prospect theory relative gains and risk acceptance can coincide, states do sometimes seek cooperation as a relative gains strategy.

In an important sense, the Montreal case presents a very low hurdle for realism and liberalism. The attempt to fix a single goal for states leaves us deaf to the empirical challenge of a world in which states exhibit a broader set of behaviors. Frequently, states pursue relative gains in one issue and absolute gains in another. Indeed, as this study attempts to understand, it is often the case that states shift between gains pursuit within a single issue. As currently developed, both realism and liberalism hold that state goals are consistent across contexts. The European Community's flip between gains pursuit serves to highlight the inherent weakness of this continuing bifurcation. While the

European Community's behavior during the Montreal Protocol negotiations escapes traditional theory, this behavior is consistent with the new framework offered here. The content of the decision frame accurately predicts community policy. In a gains frame, the EC exhibited risk aversion and absolute gains pursuit, while in a losses frame, the EC became risk acceptant and pursued relative advantage.

Chapter 7

The United States

American participation in the negotiations leading to the Montreal Protocol is similar to the European Community in that it can also be separated into two stages. The first begins with the initial discovery and dissemination of the ozone depletion hypothesis in 1974 and continues for a short period after the decision to impose a domestic ban on all nonessential CFC aerosol propellants in 1978. The second begins shortly after the ban, ending with the treaty in Montreal.

BACKGROUND

An important difference between the U.S. and EC cases lies in the processes by which a decision frame was defined. Real changes in the international political topography—first increased relative and absolute gains, then threatened U.S. sanctions, scientific consensus, and an about-face by American producers—created a new decision frame for the European Community. These factors were largely external, originating in the international system. By contrast, this chapter demonstrates that the forces shaping the decision frame for U.S. policymakers were internal—the result of a discursive shift in the domestic political debate over appropriate regulatory action.

The initial attempt to secure an international agreement languished under a reluctant international community that included the United States. Eventually, however, the United States became a strong advocate for a new ozone regime. So important was U.S. leadership that David Donniger, then senior attorney in the Washington office of the Natural Resources Defense Council—the very organization that sued the U.S. government for not adhering to its legal obligation to protect the ozone layer under the Clean Air Act—eventually declared that "the United States can be proud of its role in the negotiations. . . . the United States pressed the hardest among the world's major industrial powers for CFC and halon reductions" (Donniger 1988, 86). Despite considerable research into the causes and consequences of the Montreal Protocol, this American about-face has received little if any attention.[1]

The American move to multilateralism was motivated by a losses frame that produced a new risk-acceptant policy of cooperation. Ironically, this frame was largely the result of lobbying by the CFC industry. The crucial industry argument in defining a losses frame was not that proposed CFC regulations would hurt industry—producers made this complaint long before U.S. policy changed. Rather, a losses frame took hold only after the Alliance for Responsible CFC Policy depicted the status quo as a loss. It was then that decision makers in the United States became concerned with the American position in the international CFC trade.

The discussion below first documents the U.S. decision to ban aerosols. During this period, the issue lacked a decision frame.[2] U.S. policymakers possessed a technical rather than economic definition of the problem, and this was sustained through the period shortly following the aerosol ban.[3] Second, I discuss the domestic changes that produced a new losses frame for ozone politics in the U.S. With a change in the political definition of the status quo, American policy breaks sharply from passivity to embrace risk acceptance, negotiation, and relative gains pursuit.

BANNING CFCS PRIOR TO A DECISION FRAME

In 1974, the articulation of the ozone depletion hypothesis precipitated the onset of the "Ozone War" in the U.S., a wrenching public debate that pitted scientists, industry, and environmentalists against one another over the question of CFC regulation (Dotto and Schiff 1978). In the United States, ozone depletion was at first seen as a domestic concern and the policy debate played out primarily in congressional committees. Naive members within the House and Senate had to rely heavily upon the scientific community for an immediate set of evaluations and policy prescriptions. Meanwhile, the CFC industry, rather than emphasize the economic costs of domestic CFC regulation, instead emphasized the value of CFCs to society and challenged any scientific findings that suggested a link between CFCs and ozone depletion. This emphasis upon science short-circuited an economic definition of ozone politics from the constituency most likely to force such a discussion.

Indeed, the primary reaction within the U.S. government to the depletion hypothesis was cautious restraint. A former EPA official captures the mood well: "Never had the government been faced with such a seemingly innocuous substance causing such indirect, remote effects which would occur decades in the future, but which were not directly demonstrable at the time when control needed to be initiated" (Bastain 1982, 165). However, the threat of ecological collapse was sufficiently compelling for an initially reluctant Congress to consider new regulations. The scientific testimony presented to congressional committees was highly technical and often difficult for Congress to understand.[4] At times, scientists even found themselves amused by the simplistic manner in which government officials, unacquainted with the inherent ambiguities of ozone science, approached the issue. One senator, growing frustrated with the complexities of atmospheric chemistry, finally proclaimed, "I am not trying to put you in a box of any kind. Just give me a Yes or No answer" (Dotto and Schiff 1978, 194). The following set of questions put to a senior biologist at Brookhaven National Laboratory reflects well the desire for basic information (U.S. Congress 1975):

- Is there a direct relationship between the depth of the penetration and the intensity of the UV?
- Can you conclude from that, that the effects of UV on plant life are adverse to some degree?
- How long a period of time did it take us to discover that smog had an adverse effect on plant life?
- How long do you estimate it would take us to make this determination on the effects of UV on plants?
- Are there any good effects of UV?
- What does vitamin D do?

The hearings thus fed vital information to a knowledge-starved Congress. The discussions were not politically charged, nor were they witness to long posturing by members or panelists. Instead, the atmosphere was very workmanlike. The reaction of the CFC industry reinforced this tone. One might expect policymakers to be primarily concerned with scientific questions at an early, definitional stage. But CFC producers and users also focused their attention on scientific questions, such that "if any single theme could be said to characterize industry's pitch, it was that the Rowland and Molina theory was just that—a theory. It had not been 'proved'" (Dotto and Schiff 1978, 177). The vice president of Du Pont's Organic Chemicals Department used his time before Congress to define the scientific issues from an industry perspective, and to highlight industry's pledge of $5 million for university research to develop data necessary to make informed judgments about the relationship of

CFCs to ozone depletion. Du Pont also proclaimed its commitment to be guided by science, such that "if credible scientific data show that certain fluorocarbons cannot be used without a threat to health, Du Pont will stop production of those compounds" (U.S. Congress 1975). As the largest American producer of CFCs, Du Pont's strategy was therefore adopted by the industry as a whole.[5]

This strategy appears at first glance to be unnecessarily risky. If the scientific case against CFCs eventually proved conclusive, then Congress and the public would expect CFC producers to stop production.[6] More often, the approach by the targets of potential regulatory action is to argue that the economic costs would be unbearable. Even if such arguments do not entirely forestall government regulation, they hold the best chance of reducing its eventual costs. However, within the context of the ozone war, this traditional approach would grant the pernicious nature of CFCs, something producers very much wanted to avoid. If subsequent study proved CFCs to be a threat to the global ecosystem, the consequences of ozone destruction were such that government regulation was nearly inevitable. Industry's pledge to stop production therefore cost little. Instead, industry representatives opted to challenge any data or theory suggesting that CFCs damaged the stratospheric ozone.[7] The main thrust of these early efforts, and the more focused attempts that followed, was to undermine support for new regulation by blunting any suggestion that CFCs pose a danger to the ecological health of the planet.

When given opportunities to make its case to policy makers, the CFC industry therefore did not argue against regulation on the grounds that it would be expensive, or that it would put U.S. companies at a disadvantage. Representatives actually downplayed the potential economic consequences of a CFC ban, imploring Congress, "[P]lease do not get the impression that a fluorocarbon ban would result in permanent unemployment. . . . Other products would replace some of the fluorocarbon-dependent products, creating new jobs" (U.S. Congress 1975, 10). When asked directly if an aerosol ban would harm his company—seemingly a perfect opportunity to complain about undue regulatory burdens—the vice president of Gilette responded instead that Gilette might have difficulty meeting the increased demand for its non-aerosol products (U.S. Congress 1975, 726). The international consequences of CFC regulation were similarly downplayed. In their written statements to Congress, none of the major CFC producers—including Racon, Kaiser, Du Pont, and Union Carbide—mentioned a loss of international competitiveness as a negative consequence of unilateral action (U.S. Congress 1976, 459–476). The aerosol packaging industry did acknowledge that there was an international dimension to ozone protection, but it did not challenge the idea of a unilateral ban on the grounds that it would put the industry at a competitive disadvantage. Instead, it argued that a unilateral ban would be ineffective in protecting the ozone layer (Marriott 1975, 622–625).

It was within this discursive context that the U.S. government launched two important scientific studies. First was the Interagency Task Force on Inadvertent Modification of the Stratosphere (IMOS). Initiated in 1975, IMOS drew upon expertise from "all Federal agencies with a substantial research, policy or regulatory interest in fluorocarbons or atmospheric protection" (Bastain 1982, 170).[8] The purpose behind IMOS was to provide a vehicle for the coordinated assessment of the potential for ozone damage caused by CFCs and to provide a plan of action to federal agencies on how to best prevent ozone layer depletion. The National Academy of Sciences (NAS) conducted a second study, also initiated in early 1975, intended to review the current body of existing research and produce a summary report. IMOS completed its report first, concluding that:

> fluorocarbon releases to the environment are a legitimate cause for concern. Moreover, unless new scientific evidence is found to remove the cause for concern, it would seem necessary to restrict uses of F-11 and F-12. . . . The National Academy of Sciences is currently conducting an in-depth scientific study of man-made impacts on the stratosphere and will report its findings in less than a year. If the National Academy of Sciences study confirms the current task force assessment, it is recommended that the Federal regulatory agencies initiate rule making procedures for implementing regulations to restrict fluorocarbon use. (CEQ 1974)

This conclusion represented a broad consensus among scientists within the federal government. It was important for two reasons. First, some form of regulatory action became the default position. The burden of proof was placed upon the defenders of CFCs to demonstrate that they were not harmful to the ozone layer. If the NAS did not vindicate CFCs, then some form of CFC regulation would shortly follow. Second, the decision to regulate was to be decided on scientific, not economic, grounds. The cost of regulations was not a consideration for IMOS. The report instead approached the problem from a narrower perspective, focusing entirely upon the ecological need for and effectiveness of unilateral regulations.

The NAS report was delayed five months. When released, it concluded that the best estimate for ozone depletion was 7 percent, although the possible range was anywhere from 2 to 20 percent. While interpretations of the NAS report differed outside the government—some read it as a call for immediate regulations, others as a call for a two-year study period to gather more information—the federal interpretation was more uniform. There now existed "surprising unanimity among key government officials" that CFCs needed to be regulated (Bastain 1982, 189). Both the FDA and the EPA announced their decision to initiate regulations shortly after the report was released (U.S. Congress 1976).

There were then two reinforcing dynamics that set the early tone for ozone politics in the United States. Congress, initially lacking information, looked to scientists to define the contours of the problem. Meanwhile, CFC producers, rather than decry the costs of regulation, chose to focus their challenge on the accumulating scientific evidence documenting the link between CFCs and ozone depletion. As a result, the domestic political discussion focused exclusively upon technical questions like depletion rates, ecological harm under differing depletion scenarios, and the ecological—not economic—impact of alternative regulation schemes. The initial U.S. decision to ban CFC aerosol propellants was, then, driven largely by domestic politics and was part of a limited, earnest, and preemptive attempt to protect the ozone layer. The United States was the largest producer and consumer of CFCs, and aerosol propellants constituted the largest use in the marketplace. A unilateral aerosol ban, it was believed, would produce significant ecological benefits.[9]

It is for these reasons that the enactment of the aerosol ban did not by itself produce a losses frame among policymakers within the U.S. government. One might expect that the industry groups stung by regulation would surely revise their evaluation of the status quo and communicate their displeasure to policymakers. However, CFC producers were not complaining about the burdens of regulation, and therefore decision makers viewed CFCs as a technically complicated environmental issue and not as a politically charged decision that might damage an important constituent industry. While industry did eventually develop a highly coordinated and sophisticated lobbying effort decrying the costs of the aerosol ban, the argument did not gain widespread acceptance until after the failed talks in Vienna.

American Passivity

The American position during international meetings beginning in early 1977 demonstrates both a break between domestic and international CFC policy and the lack of a clearly defined decision frame. At the same time that Congress pressed forward with unilateral domestic regulation, U.S. delegates to the ozone talks did little or nothing on the international front. U.S. policymakers had several opportunities to push vigorously for an international agreement, but they opted instead for a posture that is best characterized as risk averse and passive.

U.S. strategy at three consecutive international conferences held in 1977 was typical. The United States hosted the first UNEP meeting in Washington, D.C., to discuss scientific issues. Here, reluctant states argued that international CFC regulation was premature and that the first step should instead coordinate various research projects to establish the veracity of the proposed link between CFCs and ozone depletion. For their part, U.S. delegates noted that the aerosol ban demonstrated clearly that the U.S. government was already convinced that CFCs posed a threat sufficient to justify regulation, but they did not push other governments to follow. Instead, the U.S. agreed to a set of recommendations for a World Plan of Action on the Ozone Layer. The document contained no binding language, timetables for reductions, nor a proposal on how to proceed with an international agreement. By all accounts, its impact "beyond that of encouragement and communication was considered minimal" (Bastain 1982, 192). It did contain a provision to consider the possibility of international cooperation in ozone research. This was a position acceptable even to the most recalcitrant governments.

An April follow-up meeting dealt explicitly with regulatory issues. Here, the United States explained its intent to enact the proposed aerosol ban and gave other participants the details of their proposed regulation.[10] Nonetheless, the United States continued to support the position that while ozone depletion was indeed a global problem, "individual nations would be making their own decisions about how, whether, and when to act to reduce fluorocarbon emissions" (Bastain 1982, 192). As there existed no strong advocate for an international treaty, a third meeting held in the Federal Republic of Germany again made little progress. The United States, well on the way toward domestic regulation of aerosol propellants, continued to argue that ozone depletion was best addressed by independent unilateral efforts.[11] At the same time that it moved forward with domestic regulation, the United States permitted international efforts to sputter.

As a result, during this early period, the United States approached the domestic regulation of CFCs as an issue having little bearing on international competitiveness. At international conferences, the United States consistently supported only the weakest of proposals, unwilling to confront recalcitrant states and urge them to adopt measures that the United States was imposing domestically. However, shortly after the implementation of a unilateral aerosol ban in 1978, U.S. representatives reversed course, emphasizing international competitiveness and pushing very hard for an international ozone agreement. This reversal took place despite the facts that the international context remained largely unchanged, the relevant domestic political actors remained the same, and the costs of the aerosol ban were actually less than anticipated. Instead, it was the tactics of the CFC industry that changed, and this produced a new decision frame for policymakers.

THE ALLIANCE FOR CFCS

In response to the aerosol ban, industry reorganized against further restrictions and adopted a lobbying strategy intended to define the consequences of proposed new regulation in economic terms. One unintended consequence of this strategy was that it redefined the status quo as a loss. In terms familiar to prospect theory, industry efforts forced a discursive distinction between the status quo and the reference point. With a detrimental status quo now evaluated against a preban reference, a losses frame took hold that spurred a more aggressive and risk-acceptant U.S. posture at the talks.

The creation of a losses frame was not immediate. With the decision to ban nonessential aerosol propellants, domestic policy makers confronted the problem of implementation. Because CFC propellants were found in many products, they were subject to several different regulatory agencies. For the sake of coordination and efficiency, Congress amended the Clean Air Act in 1977 and gave the EPA broad authority over ozone regulation. It also charged the EPA chief with promulgating new regulations when, in his judgment, any substance, practice, process, or activity may reasonably be anticipated to endanger public health or welfare. The EPA used this authority to pursue further restrictions of CFCs beyond propellants. In October 1980, the EPA published its Advanced Notice of Proposed Rulemaking (ANPR). The purpose of the ANPR was to collect public reaction to a set of new regulatory options for expanding the ban on CFCs. The various options differed somewhat in scope, timing, and form, but all would have further restricted the legal domestic uses of CFCs.

Stung by what they perceived to be the unreasonable and unwarranted banning of CFC aerosol propellants and fearful of this new threat from the EPA, CFC producers and consumers under the leadership of Du Pont formed the Alliance for Responsible CFC Policy. The industry had "been staggering from disaster to disaster," and its public image was "in tatters" (Dotto and Schiff 1978, 155). The function of the alliance was to act as the official spokesman for over five hundred businesses, providing much needed coordination for an industry-wide campaign against further regulation. It presented a united front intended to "convince the government—Congress, the White House and anyone else—that the EPA's proposal to restrict CFCs is ill-advised" (Roan 1989, 103).

In addition to continuing industry's assault on the scientific foundations for a CFC ban, the alliance now gave equal time to the potential economic costs of further restrictions. The industry tested its new arguments during the next round of congressional hearings in July 1981, convened to discuss the ANPR. With a new emphasis on the economic impact of regulation, the alliance argued that any new restrictions would "impose substantial and adverse economic impacts upon producers and users of CFCs and upon American workers and consumers" (U.S. Congress 1981b, 83). Alliance lobbying prior to the hearings had already softened up Congress, which was by now as much concerned with the economic impact of EPA proposals as it was with ozone depletion. Indeed, congressional representatives praised industry representatives for their efforts in bringing the pernicious nature of regulations into the light.[12] The nonpolitical and workmanlike tone that characterized previous hearings had evaporated. Industry representatives argued that EPA proposals would produce both increasing unemployment and business failure. All sectors of the alliance chimed in, including both small and large firms. Typical were the comments from the owner of a small air-conditioning firm who complained the ANPR embodied proposals that would impose "more economic hardship that I believe my company can withstand," while the larger Whirlpool Corporation claimed the EPA proposals would result in "lower employment" and "devastating" economic ripple effects (U.S. Congress 1981b, 8, 17). EPA representatives countered that the agency was fully cognizant of the economic impact of additional regulations; however, members of Congress dismissed the claim with statements like "I would love to believe that. . . . But the agency's record speaks for itself" (U.S. Congress 1981b, 60). Whereas Congress once looked to federal agencies and the scientific community for technical information, they now attacked these same groups for their insensitivity to economic considerations.

Under increasing pressure, the EPA backpedaled. A year earlier, the deputy administrator of the EPA announced at an international meeting in Oslo, Norway, that the United States intended to go beyond the aerosol ban to regulate other applications (Blum 1981, 58–59). The ANPR was intended to be the first step in this next round of restrictions. Under the weight of Alliance and congressional attacks, the EPA reclassified ANPR as a simple information-gathering device and declared that it in no way meant that the EPA intended to go forward with more regulation. Proregulatory groups like the Natural Resources Defense Council were left lamenting that the focus of the discussion had shifted to the economic costs of regulations and ignored the potentially significant ecological benefits. Indeed, there was considerable doubt among virtually all environmental groups that the issue could be resolved before serious damage to the environment occurred.[13]

Importantly, while the alliance's economic argument refocused the domestic political debate, it did not yet define a new decision frame for policymakers. The status quo and reference point both still represented current conditions. The alliance redefined ozone protection in economic terms, but its success in lobbying against future regulations meant that the status quo was secure, and that the CFC industry was free from the costs of future regulation. Alliance opposition to an international agreement was then simply an extension of its strategy with respect to domestic regulation. An international agreement would lend legitimacy to the assertion that CFCs posed a real threat to the environment. This was something the CFC industry wanted to avoid—even if it meant that other countries were permitted to continue producing and consuming the very aerosol propellants that had been banned in the U.S. If the notion that CFCs damaged the ozone layer was accepted, there was no logical limit to restricting their use short of banning them altogether.

This emphasis on scientific and economic concerns over ecological issues short-circuited enthusiasm for an international treaty within the U.S. government, which was by now sympathetic to the assertion that further regulations would harm industry. For policymakers, an international agreement was also viewed as risky because it would grant the argument that CFCs were an environmental menace and likely open the door to further and deeper international restrictions on CFC production and use. Accordingly, the U.S. blocked attempts to secure a treaty while many other states were moving toward the idea of an international agreement. For example, the U.S. rejected a plan offered by Finland and Sweden—the Nordic Annex—calling for an international aerosol ban. The EC and Japan were also strongly against such a measure, arguing that the economic costs were too high and that current data suggested such drastic measures were not needed (Litfin 1994, 74). Of course, this was not the case for the United States, which had already instituted a ban. Nonetheless, the United States refused to become a party to the proposal. U.S. representatives raised the narrow technical objection that a framework convention must precede any discussion of control measures. Because no participant—the United States included—had offered a convention proposal, the United States could not accede to an annex. Without a strong advocate from a significant producing country, the annex died, and the U.S. reaffirmed its position that the best way to address the issue was for each state to craft its own set of unilateral regulations.

AN INADVERTENT LOSSES FRAME

The new alliance strategy emphasizing the economic consequences of additional regulation reshaped policymaker perceptions of the status quo, though this was not necessarily intended. The economic arguments against further regulation eventually forced a reevaluation of the past consequences of the aerosol ban. This created a discursive distinction between current conditions that were detrimental to business and the favorable preban conditions. The issue first came up in the early 1980s before the House Committee on Energy and Commerce. The committee was considering further amendments to the Clean Air Act. In his testimony before Congress, the director of Du Pont's freon division complained that other nations had not followed America's lead: "Unilateral action has historically been the EPA's basic approach. With its CFC aerosol ban, the United States already has gone far beyond action taken by any other major CFC-producing or consuming country. In contrast, the EEC has only reduced aerosol usage by 30 percent" (U.S. Congress 1981a, 443). The intended point here was that unilateral domestic legislation would fail to protect the global environment. However, this lament, combined with the alliance's concern over the potential harm of further domestic regulations, was quickly honed into a new argument. Not only did the rest of the world fail to follow the U.S. lead to protect the environment, that fact also put American industry at a competitive disadvantage. With preban conditions as an anchor, industry went on to make the case that U.S. domestic firms currently suffered because of past unilateral action: "[T]he experience with the US aerosol propellant ban should teach us that unilateral domestic action without agreement on a global approach will not resolve this issue, but will . . . cause a US loss of world market share for goods and services and further increase trade deficits" (Blanchard 1987, 194).

The international consequences of U.S. domestic regulation now took center stage in the debate, and a losses frame began to permeate all branches of government. The State Department, which had remained silent on the issue until now, internalized the alliance argument in suggesting that "when we [the US] took unilateral action on aerosols, banning CFCs for aerosols, some years ago, the rest of the world did, in fact, sit back and let our industry take the brunt of it" (U.S. Congress 1987, 24). Members of Congress, the EPA, and even proregulatory environmental groups now all expressed a concern for the damage done to U.S. industry by past unilateral action. Even the World Resources Institute, an organization that aggressively promoted further regulation, began to modify its position. Understanding that industry's complaint about the burden of past regulations resonated with policymakers, the institute declared that the policy of the United States should be to pursue regulations that do not impose severe economic costs on American industry.

Initially, the discussion about CFCs focused primarily upon the narrow technical issues of atmospheric chemistry or (more recently) the domestic economic impact of additional regulation. During this period, for reasons outlined above, status quo conditions were not evaluated against the past. That is, the status quo and the reference point both represented current conditions. However, as the alliance argument that the aerosol ban hurt U.S. industry took hold, the status quo was increasingly compared against preban conditions and considered to be a loss.

Decision makers within government now operated under a losses frame and proved willing to risk international cooperation in an attempt to return to preban conditions. The choice set confronting U.S. policymakers closely resembles that given in earlier chapters for states in a losses frame. Continued American passivity (accepting the status quo) meant accepting certain current losses. International cooperation represented a gamble. It could produce further loss, but it also contained the possibility of recovering lost ground. Pursuing international cooperation represented a gamble because it might lay the foundation for a more complete ban on CFCs—which did in fact happen— and this would be even more damaging to domestic CFC producers. However, it also held the potential to mitigate the damage now perceived to have resulted from the aerosol ban. In the end, the U.S. opted to risk cooperation in an attempt to return to the preban reference point.[14]

THE MOVE TO MULTILATERALISM: VIENNA AND MONTREAL

Until 1985, the United States had been reluctant to take a strong international position, opting instead to defer to reluctant states. However, when the parties reconvened in Vienna, the United States began pushing aggressively for a binding international protocol that would commit states to significant CFC reductions. That is, American policy shifted dramatically from international passivity to pursuing relative advantage through multilateral agreement. Not quite two years after the failed Nordic Annex, Canada, Norway, and Switzerland joined Finland and Sweden to form the Toronto Group and reintroduced the notion of an aerosol ban. Presented again with a proposal that it had previously rejected, the United States, now under a losses frame, joined the Toronto Group. The group also proposed that a convention for the elimination of aerosol propellants be drafted. The United States agreed, declaring that "the margin of error between complacency and catastrophe is too small for comfort" (U.S. Department of State 1985).

Under U.S. prodding, the Toronto Group also developed a new set of proposals for a CFC protocol. This "multioption" approach would allow states to choose one of four alternative control schemes. All of the alternatives targeted aerosols either by explicitly demanding aerosol cuts or by demanding general reductions such that aerosol substitutes would have to be developed (Sand 1985). The set of proposals to which the United States was now party had one common element. None required further U.S. cuts, but would require them of the European Community. A far cry from past unilateral action in which the international consequences of banning were not even considered, the United States was now only willing to entertain proposals which promised that U.S. industry would reclaim lost ground.

U.S. officials argued that their position reflected nothing more than an earnest attempt to protect the ozone layer, but recent findings in the scientific community did not support this contention. While a global aerosol ban would secure a short-term reduction in global emissions, growth in other sectors of the economy would quickly undo any gains from an aerosol ban.[15] The real target of U.S. efforts was Europe. This statement by a U.S. delegate is typical:

> It is important in any control regime that we have in the United States that American industry not be disadvantaged, and that is precisely why we are engaged in these international negotiations, because unlike eight or nine years ago when we acted unilaterally, we want this time to have the whole world, the major producers and the major user countries together agree on an international mechanism. . . . we want within that mechanism to assure a level playing field, that US industry would not be disadvantaged by unfair competition from other countries, which are not taking the issue as seriously. (U.S. Congress 1987, 18,)

Recall from chapter 6 that the United States and the EC failed to agree at Vienna. The major obstacle in that case was determining the method by which CFC emissions were to be calculated. Under a losses frame, the United States was unwilling to concede to the EC's proposal that would fix the status quo through multilateral agreement. Instead, the United States favored an "adjusted production" approach to measure reductions that required greater cuts in EC exports. The U.S. position reflects an attempt to deny EC producers the relative gains in global market share enjoyed because of the unilateral aerosol ban. The main consequence of the adjusted production approach was that it would equalize production and export levels between the EC and the United States, while a simple production freeze would not require the EC to give up its position as the dominant international supplier.

Congress communicated this desire directly to the U.S. negotiating team. In response, diplomats assured Congress that they were "trying very hard . . . to keep the international negotiations and the domestic processes on a parallel track," and that the team was operating under "a forcing date of mid-September for a diplomatic convention" (U.S. Congress 1987).[16] The combination of concern about court-ordered deadlines and international competitiveness is even evidenced in the position of Lee Thomas, head of the EPA, who was charged to implement domestic regulation: "I think we need to look at the question [of domestic regulation] in the context of where we are internationally. I think there is no question that we need an international agreement. I look back to 1978 when we took unilateral action in the United States to ban CFCs in propellants, and, in fact, I saw very few countries follow suit" (Thomas 1987, 137). This concern for the international implications of domestic regulation is striking when compared to earlier U.S. positions. Before the establishment of a losses frame, little attention was paid to the international consequences of CFC regulation. Despite several opportunities to raise the issue during ongoing international discussions, the United States instead let those discussions founder while it went ahead with its own domestic regulations. However, after the formation of a losses frame, the United States adopted an aggressive international position promoting international cooperation. The various branches of government organized around the principle that past relative decline must be remedied and that any further domestic regulations at the very least must not result in relative decline. To this end, the United States latched onto international talks as a way of pursuing these two goals.

CONCLUSION

Several alternative explanations for the U.S. break from passivity to multilateralism can be dismissed. First, the important players remained constant throughout the talks. There were no newly interested states forcing the United States into support for a treaty, nor did the United States change policy because of shifting international coalitions or alliances. Second, Republicans took control of the White House in 1980, suggesting that the push for international regulations did not come from a favorable shift in governmental ideology. The Reagan administration was largely antiregulatory in its philosophy. Finally, the objective national interests of the United States did not appreciably change. Ozone protection never became an issue of national security,[17] nor did the fundamental economic issues change much after the initial effects of the aerosol ban took hold.

What did change was the political definition of the status quo. Many domestic issues have international consequences, and this was true for ozone protection. The point here is not simply that industry felt that more regulation would be costly. The alliance had articulated this argument to policymakers in a successful attempt to forestall a planned second round of regulations by the EPA. During this period, U.S. international policy remained unchanged. It was not until the political discourse of loss took hold that the United States moved to a policy of international cooperation and relative gains pursuit.

The U.S. case thus also provides an important counterpoint to the EC with respect to the origins of the decision frame, demonstrating that frames are defined both by international system and domestic forces. Defining the status quo as a loss was not a first strategy for the alliance, but industry's antiregulatory efforts did create that result. A losses frame was not in any sense inevitable, and therefore neither was an agreement in Montreal. There is an irony here. One possible unintended consequence of interest group lobbying against domestic legislation is that such efforts can actually increase the likeli-

hood of international regulation. If the proposed regulations have some precedent (like the aerosol ban), one common antiregulatory strategy is to highlight
the economic consequences of the precedent regulation. The effect of this may
be to establish a losses frame in the regulatory discourse. The onset of a losses
frame motivates risk acceptant behavior, sometimes manifesting itself in the
pursuit of a gamble to secure a favorable international agreement. This is an
outcome that, presumably, domestic antiregulatory groups would lament.

There is a significant body of research suggesting that domestic politics
are at least as important as international dynamics in understanding foreign
policy outcomes. Indeed, some have argued that domestic explanations are
more important. Because U.S. participation in the Montreal Protocol presents
us with a case in which changes in the domestic political topography emerge
as the important factors in defining the decision frame, we are provided with
an opportunity to investigate prospect theory's traction onto the domestic
dimensions of international politics. Still, the framework offered here is agnostic with respect to the relative importance of international versus domestic factors. Chapter 3 left the location for definition of the decision frame to
empirical investigation; it is not theoretically prespecified. The U.S. example
demonstrates that there is no theoretic imperative that the definitions of the
decision frame are only imposed externally, as was the case for the European
Community.

Chapter 8

Conclusions

The discussion presented in chapters 6 and 7 can not test all of the propositions developed in this book. However, an examination of the Montreal Protocol demonstrates that prospect theory does meet the challenge outlined for it in chapter 1. It is possible to connect the various subfields of international relations using cognitive psychology to explain important aspects of state behavior. The previous two chapters provide evidence for an integrated framework that describes the origin and content of state preferences, the propensity of states to accept or decline risk, the conditions conducive for international cooperation, and the unintentional consequences of power. This chapter further develops the implications of prospect theory in the context of established theories for studying international relations.

PREFERENCES AND FRAMES

Chapter 5 connected preferences over gains to the decision frame. For the EC, a decision frame was defined by changes in the international political topography that were largely beyond its control. The EC frame shifted from gains to losses, and with this shift, EC policy changed from absolute to relative gains pursuit. Such flips in preference are not possible under the current debate between realism and liberalism. In the U.S. case, discursive changes created a losses decision frame where previously no frame existed. This suggests that the set of conditions which define decision frames—and in turn, motivate choices—are not always objective. By explaining both EC and U.S. behavior, prospect theory highlights the importance of looking to both real and subjective factors in the definition of the decision frame.

The finding that frame definition can originate from changes in international or domestic politics also supports the argument that the ongoing debate between domestic versus international explanations is counterproductive. However, the framework provided here offers no guidance concerning where to look first, and this can be considered a weakness in the approach. Under prospect theory, frame definition is not a theoretical issue; it is instead an empirical question best answered from within the context of each case.

REALISM AND COOPERATION

Realism argues that change in relative position will undermine cooperation. An important conclusion of this study is that risk disposition can overcome the corrosive effect that relative gains is thought to have on cooperation. Chapter 4 demonstrated that under a losses frame states will risk cooperation even when the expected outcome is further loss. Chapter 5 argued that sensitivity to relative position increases under conditions of loss. Combined, these arguments suggest that, contrary to realism, loss can produce risk-acceptant attempts to secure cooperation, and that this is part of a relative gains strategy.

Recall that the exit costs associated with abandoning formal negotiations midstream, combined with the fact that the eventual outcome of a negotiated endeavor is ultimately unknown, means the decision to enter into negotiations is often viewed by governments as a gamble. The decision to negotiate an ozone treaty contained considerable uncertainty and risks for both the United States and EC. There was strong disagreement over how best to define CFC emissions. Under a losses frame, and consistent with realism, both the United States and the EC promoted a definition that would minimize the chance of relative decline. Ultimately, a compromise divided emissions into two parts: production, defined as the amount produced minus the amount destroyed, and consumption, defined as domestic production plus imports.[1] This compromise had important implications for the EC. Because it was exporting a third of its production in 1986, the EC could continue to produce more CFCs than it would use domestically, while EC client states would have to reduce imports in order to comply.[2] The EC would therefore continue to sell excess CFCs to states that were not party to the protocol. Most important here were large developing nations that lacked adequate production capacity, but were projected to have rapidly increasing demand.

If large numbers of developing states did not sign the protocol, then the EC would remain the dominant supplier to global markets. If a majority did sign, then the restrictions on imports would dry up EC markets. Neither the

United States nor the EC knew how many other states would eventually join and, therefore, which side would eventually secure the largest relative gains.[3] The depiction of cooperation as constituting a gamble therefore applies here, and it was only under a losses frame that each side—at different times depending upon the onset of the losses frame—chose to gamble on a negotiated settlement. The preference for relative gains—also produced by a losses frame—did not inhibit cooperation as realism would predict. Instead, it was an appetite for relative gains that ultimately brought both the United States and the EC to the negotiating table.

Still, this analysis does demonstrate that relative gains concerns do emerge between governments—even in issue areas not typically thought to impinge on state security. This confirms realist claims that their perspective is not limited to so-called high politics, and that we should no longer simply assume that liberalism is the best choice when studying low politics. It also undermines the conventional wisdom that both liberalism and realism are correct, but that they are best applied to economic and security domains respectively. U.S. and EC behavior demonstrates instead that neither preference is universal, that such preferences are contextually bound, and that they are at least partially determined by decision maker evaluations of the status quo.

RISK ACCEPTANCE, COOPERATION, AND REGIME DESIGN

Chapter 4 demonstrated how risk acceptance can lead states to accept new regime rules that leave them open to exploitation. States under a losses frame are therefore more willing to accept incomplete monitoring and verification schemes than are states operating under gains. Such behavior is risky because it opens the state to exploitation by noncooperators. The compromise between the United States and the EC on the status of the yet uncommitted developing counties extends this argument into the domain of regime membership. Risk acceptance pushed both the United States and EC to commit to the Montreal Protocol even though it was clear that several important countries—China and India among them—might ultimately decline, leaving themselves bound to costly restrictions while large developing states continue increasing levels production and consumption unabated.

Here again, both sides attempted to reduce this risk in a way that served their interests, but neither could sufficiently bend the process entirely to their interests. Late in the negations, the EC became a strong advocate for the special circumstances of developing nations and successfully pushed for exceptions that permitted time lags for full compliance should they join. The intent here was to assure that even if they did join the protocol, developing nations would be allowed to continue imports for several years. The United States pushed trade provisions that provided incentives to join, initially proposing an outright ban on exports to nonparties. This would have eliminated the benefits to the EC of domestic overproduction (Benedick 1991, 91). For this reason, the U.S. proposal was strongly opposed by the EC. Both sides eventually forged a compromise that would allow exports to nonparties until 1993, after which exports would be counted against domestic consumption. However, this did not settle the issue as many developing states continued to negotiate for still more favorable terms—for example, longer compliance lags and technology transfers—as additional conditions for their participation.

POWER, LEVERAGE, AND DOMESTIC WIN-SETS

Prospect theory also sheds new light on the application of power in negotiated settings. Power can alter decision maker frames and thereby risk disposition and gains preference. The conventional understanding of power as a tool to circumscribe rival action is now supplemented with the notion that power can inadvertently alter the content of rival policy goals in predictable ways. The threat embodied in U.S.-proposed trade legislation helped shape a losses frame for the EC. The shift for the EC was from gains to losses, and thus from absolute to relative gains pursuit. While not explored in this analysis, it follows that the application of power through rewards can also change the decision frame for the target from losses to gains and, therefore, its policy goals from relative to absolute gains pursuit. This new dimension to the application of power bears further examination.

Moreover, revisions to Putnam's original two-level framework in addition to those discussed in chapter 3 are supported by evidence in the Montreal Case. The issue is whether having a narrow, inflexible domestic win-set provides negotiators leverage in their attempts to get rival states to agree to terms. The notion is a venerable one. Its origins lie in Thomas Schelling's powerfully simple argument that, in negotiated settings, it is often to the benefit of either party to appear immobile. Governments confronted with a bound and immobile negotiating partner must either acquiesce or abandon the attempt to secure an agreement. However, a declaration of immobility produces leverage only if negotiating partners view the claim to be credible. Recent research conducted under the two-level framework has suggested otherwise: that rivals instead view the claim of immobility as a bargaining position rather than a meaningful constraint. Research demonstrates that often rivals do not buy the argument that their negotiating partners are incapacitated by powerful domestic actors (Evans 1993, 402). As a result, "the 'tying-hands' strategy, suggested by Thomas Schelling's work, is logically plausible but lacks efficacy" in actual negotiations (Evans 1993, 399).

The analysis offered here at first seems to further cloud the issue. In the case of the European Community, the Commission was in fact constrained by the strictures given to it under the original negotiating mandate. However, this immobility did not translate into effective leverage over the United States. Instead, the widespread perception of immobility actually hurt EC credibility. As the negotiations deadlocked, the EC was viewed as stubbornly shortsighted in its defense of domestic CFC production and incapable of negotiating as a single decision-making unit on issues in which its constituent states were not in complete agreement. By contrast, U.S. negotiators successfully pressed the EC into serious negotiations in large part by suggesting that the demands of domestic groups—including Congress and domestic industry—tied their hands even when this in fact overstated such constraints. The question arises as to why the perception of a limited and immobile win-set was helpful to the United States, while the reality of commission immobility did not similarly benefit the EC.

The important distinction here is between a limited win-set alone and one that is tied to changes in the status quo. While the commission operated under a limited win-set, for the United States the implications of EC immobility were only that it was immobile. In contrast, the constraints on U.S. negotiators also threatened the status quo in the form of domestic trade legislation. U.S. immobility thus contributed to a losses frame for the EC, while EC immobility had little bearing upon decision maker perceptions of the status quo in the United States. The losses frame produced by U.S. immobility meant that the EC was more willing to gamble on a negotiated settlement.

The traditional view of policy makers under the two-level approach is that they are forced to balance domestic and international concerns. It emphasizes the strategic environment in which leaders find themselves and the trade-offs available to them. While essentially correct, this largely ignores the play of power. It is for this reason that empirical research on two-level games could not identify the conditions under which immobility provides a strategic advantage. Substituting prospect theory for rationality in the two-level framework suggests a new set of dynamics by which immobility produces leverage. Key here is the impact of immobility upon rival assessments of the status quo.

THE "OZONE HOLE"

Finally, my analysis of U.S. and EC behavior agrees with the common view that a concern for ecological stability initially prompted the dissemination and discussion of the ozone depletion hypothesis and pushed ozone layer protection onto the international political scene. However, it also demonstrates that the compelling issues in securing a treaty were economic, not environmental.

As noted earlier, there existed no empirical evidence outside the laboratory to prove that CFCs were in fact destroying the ozone layer. More importantly, the scientific consensus at the time was that the control provisions of the Montreal Protocol would do little to forestall an ecological catastrophe if the link between CFCs and depletion did in fact exist (Doolittle 1989). One observer puzzled, "Why, when professionals cannot make up their minds even about what is happening in the Antarctic, should the World's diplomats be locked in negotiations?" (Maddox 1987, 101). The picture that emerges from this study is that what was at first an ecological issue quickly became dominated by economic concerns. Previous research has largely ignored the economic roots of the U.S. and EC disagreement.[4] For this reason, a focus on gains preference and risk predisposition captures the essence of the struggle to get an ozone treaty.

Nonetheless, an economic discussion of the Montreal Protocol confronts the so-called ozone hole over Antarctica. The discovery of the hole is often given credit for the treaty in Montreal. The common view is that its emergence constituted the final nail in the scientific coffin for CFCs, providing those who argued on scientific grounds that a treaty was needed with proof of the consequences of inaction (Litfin 1994). By this view, the ozone hole constituted a "powerful symbol of the potential for global catastrophe" and, as a result "galvanized world opinion on the need for international measures to protect the ozone layer" (Morrisette 1989, 154).

There are at least three reasons to question the argument that the ozone hole was primarily responsible for the Montreal Protocol. First, from the time of its discovery to the signing of the final agreement, the scientific community had no explanation for the ozone hole.[5] It was not predicted in any atmospheric models, and there was no consensus as to whether it represented a human produced pathology or a natural seasonal effect, nor whether the cause was chemical or atmospheric. Second, all parties agreed not to discuss the hole during negations, and the ozone hole was neither addressed at the talks nor used by participants as a justification for or against a treaty.[6] The United States feared that the hole might be caused by atmospherics and that the need for a treaty that would harmonize domestic and international regulations would be called into question. The EC feared that the cause might be chemical and would strengthen the argument for more stringent global restrictions. Finally, as noted earlier, if the ozone hole was a powerful representation of catastrophic ecological collapse, we would expect that the final agreement would enact measures at least sufficient to save the planet. It did not. Ozone depletion was expected to continue under the terms agreed to at Montreal.[7]

The Promise of a Cognitive Research Program

The study of international politics firmly "grounded in the assumptions and knowledge of cognitive actors" is increasingly offered as fertile territory for the creation of new international relations theory (Rosati 2001, 45). Nonmaximizing decision rules probably evolved and survived because they proved useful to individuals in integrating complex information. Such strategies are then cognitive fixtures and part of a shared evolutionary legacy (Cosmides 1989). This is not to suggest that rationalist theory has run its course—new theoretical innovations emerge constantly. However, rational choice theory continues parallel to empirical findings from the study of human decision making that, in principle at least, undermine the foundations of the rationalist program.

There is a good deal more theoretical and empirical work that will need to be completed before cognitive theories of international politics can legitimately claim to offer a comprehensive alternative to traditional rationalist theory. The application of prospect theory to issues not discussed here remains unexplored terrain. There is also a wealth of empirical work in cognitive psychology, beyond prospect theory, that can be fruitfully mined by students of international politics. Much of this work is equally compelling, but perhaps less circulated among political scientists.

Notes

Notes for Chapter 1

1. For a summary of major findings see Kahneman, Slovic, and Tversky 1982 and Bell, Raffa, and Tversky 1988. For a good nontechnical summary see Plous 1993.

2. Morgenthau's (1960, part 1) statement on the role of rationality assumptions in international relations theory remains the cornerstone for this position.

3. For a summary discussion of the increasing role of cognitive psychology in economics see Economist 1999. For a discussion of the role of prospect theory in the creation of the new field of behavioral economics, see Laibson 1998.

4. See for example Vertzberger 1990.

5. For a good review of constructivism in international relations see Alder 1997. For an attempt to infuse the constructvist program with a theory of agency see Berejikian and Dryzek 2000.

6. Given the many good expositions in the literature, my discussion only summarizes prospect theory. For complete description see for example, Kahneman and Tversky 1979; McDermott 1998 (chap 2); and Quatrone and Tversky 1988.

7. The implications of a subjectively constituted decisional frame will be discussed in later chapters.

8. Under rational choice individuals maximize by weighting the utility of an outcome by its probability. Under prospect theory, the value of a prospect is multiplied by a decision weight. Values on the weighting curve increase with probability but are a nonlinear function of probabilities. Specifically, low probabilities are overweighted while high probabilities are underweighted. In the domain of gains, underweighting highly probably events leads to risk aversion by reducing the attractiveness of gambles that promise near certain gains, while at the same time producing risk acceptance in the domain of losses by reducing the sting of gambles promising near certain losses. Conversely, in the domain of gains, overweighting low probability events increases the value of long-shot gambles and can produce risk acceptance. In the domain of losses, overweighting low probability losses can produce risk aversion. For an extended discussion see Tversky and Kahneman 1986.

9. For a full discussion see Tversky and Kahneman 1986 and Tversky, Slovic, and Kahneman 1990.

10. See for example Rothman and Slovey 1997 on the importance of message framing in selection of medical treatment; Yaniv 1999 for the impact of prospect theory on taxpayer compliance; Berger 1998 for the uses of prospect theory in advertising; and Lee 1994 for the impact of losses frames on firm expenditures.

Notes for Chapter 2

1. The research is quite clear on this point. For a concise review, see Frey and Eichenberger 1989.

2. For a comprehensive review see Kegley and Raymond 1994.

3. This is especially true in the nuclear age, where the threat of territorial war is greatly reduced.

4. For a discussion of bounded rationality see Jones 1999.

5. For a detailed discussion on the difference between substantive and procedural rationality see Simon 1985.

6. This ambiguity diminishes accountability if the advice turns out to be wrong Erve and Cohen 1990.

7. For a comprehensive review of research on framing effects and patient medical decisions without precise numerical representations of probability see Rothman and Slovey 1997.

8. This also leaves processes by which actors adopt decision frames as an empirical matter. This is not something that prospect theory is designed to predict, though the empirical chapters to follow do shed some light on how framing takes place.

9. Here again, where there is no shared decision frame, traditional bargaining theory may be more helpful in understanding the group's decisions. However, where group members share goals and decision frames, the case for prospect theory is stronger

10. For additional discussion on prospect theory and sunk costs, see Schaubroeck 1994.

11. Of course, where the probability of military success is very high, the use of force is not risky. Neither is it difficult to explain.

12. For a discussion in which both risk-acceptant and risk-averse behavior is observed, see Berejikian 1997.

13. Farnham's (1992) discussion of the Munich Crisis offers a similar analysis.

14. Such a threat need not necessarily come from an adversary, rival, or competitor. Theoretically, any external threat to A's newly updated status quo would trigger risk acceptance.

15. The best evidence that Moscow did not want a broader conflict into which it might become embroiled is clearly revealed by Soviet behavior after conflict erupted.

During the war Egypt asked for weapons, but Moscow declined and Soviet policy-makers energetically pursued a quick resolution of the dispute.

16. Further evidence for this dynamic can be found in Latin America, where political leaders found support for risky liberal reforms when societal groups operated under a losses frame (Weyland 1996).

17. These included Japanese concerns about the quality of U.S. education, corporate reliance upon individuals, the health of some U.S. firms, and economic costs of debt financing (Mastanduno 1993).

18. From the American perspective, Israeli retaliation carried the largest risks as it might split the anti-Iraqi coalition.

NOTES FOR CHAPTER 3

1. For a further discussion on anchoring see Wright and Anderson 1989.

2. As the discussion of existing research in chapter 2 suggests, most of the scholarship focuses upon the first set of conditions. The second set thus constitutes a target of opportunity for students of international politics.

3. As discussed earlier in chapter 2, much rational-choice international-relations theory focuses upon procedural rather than substantive rationality. Goals are assumed, and remain largely stable. Observed changes in behavior are thus a result of changes in expectations and probabilities. The precedent is so well established that it serves in major textbooks as the foundation for teaching international affairs to university students. See for example Bueno de Mesquita 2000. The analysis offered below follows this precedent. The origin for goals is analyzed in chapter 5.

4. Recent innovations in rational-deterrence theory have moved beyond 2x2 games (e.g.,Fearon 1997; Nalebuff 1991). However, simple 2x2 games are the foundation for modern innovations, and it is a reconsideration of foundations that is the purpose of this book.

5. Lebow and Stein (1987) also argue that traditional deterrence theory has largely ignored the distinction between strategic necessity and avarice as distinct motivations. States may seek advantage in deterrent games because they find current conditions to be unacceptable, or they may act to improve their condition even though they are satisfied with the status quo.

6. A similar analysis explains Japanese policies prior to World War II (Lebow and Stein 1987).

7. There is an important caveat to this analysis. At the extremes of very low probabilities or for very great losses framing effects break down. Given the implications of nuclear warfare, the costs of upsetting the status quo are potentially so large that they undermine framing effects. This suggests that the dynamics of nuclear and conventional deterrence may be quite different.

8. Economic threats are also used against rivals in so-called high politics. The following argument would apply to this set of interactions as well.

9. For a rebuttal see Elliott 1998.

10. Yet a third explanation involves selection bias in the research on sanctions. Scholars look to instances of imposed sanctions to determine the degree of compliance. Removed from this set are those cases where implicit threats actually induce compliance. The remaining set of cases are therefore those wherein there is already a decent chance of sanctions failing.

NOTES FOR CHAPTER 4

1. In terms of two-level games, the process of negotiations alters the domestic win-set. In addition, it may be that the reputational costs inhibit states from recklessly abandoning negotiations once committed to the process.

2. Subsequent sections define the conditions under which cooperation constitutes a risky strategy.

3. See for example, van Assen (1990), Dedreu and McCusker, 1997, and Sinjders and Raub 1998.

4. For a discussion see Keohane 1983 and Stein 1983.

5 Recent research has also demonstrated that the magnitudes of fear and temptation are also important, as are the ratios between these values (Mulford and Berejikian 2002).

6. This chapter follows the convention established in chapter 3 wherein cell values represent interval payoffs. Larger positive numbers represent increasing levels of satisfaction over the status quo while increasing negative values represent increasing dissatisfaction with outcomes. Also, an iterated game is assumed throughout.

7. Unless, of course, free-riding is widespread.

8. For example, Brewer and Kramer (1986) identified the conditions under which individuals will contribute more to commons protection than to the creation of public goods. Sell and Son (1997) find that individuals treat the decision to contribute to a public good as distinct from the decision to refrain from taking. van Dijk and Wilke (1995) also found that when individuals began with asymmetrical initial asset positions, they gave to collective endeavors in proportion to their positions, while they refrained from taking in a way that tended to equalize asymmetry in the outcome.

NOTES FOR CHAPTER FIVE

1. For ease of reading, I will interchangeably use "realism" and "neorealism," and "liberalism" and "neoliberalism." For examples of realism see Gilpin (1981, 1987); Grieco (1988, 1990); Krasner (1991); and Waltz (1979). Liberal authors include Axelrod (1984); Axelrod and Keohane (1985); Keohane (1984); and Stein (1983). The dis-

cussion of realism and liberalism which follows is not comprehensive, and thus does not identify all of the participants in the debate. Instead, I will emphasize disputes over the correct description of state goals as it relates to the question of when states find cooperation an attractive strategy.

2. See for example the discussion among, Grieco (1993), Powell (1993), and Snidal (1993).

3. For example, the debate has spilled over into other related fields such as economics (Taylor 1994), institutional behavior (Nichols 1996), environmental politics (Barkin and Shambaugh 1996), law (Abbott 1999), policy (Costello 1996), and negotiation theory (Hopmann 1995).

4. For a balanced discussion of constructivist approaches to the study of international relations, see Alder 1997.

5. For a discussion, see Jervis 1978. Jervis also makes the point that actors often subjectivly transform incentive structure. This implies a distinction between real and effective incentive structures: while operating under a PD (real matrix), states may be playing another game (effective matrix). This further undermines the liberal claim that observed cooperation is de facto evidence that states seek absolute gains.

6. The abstraction "units" can apply to any dimension of cooperation: increased trade, GNP, military might, and so on.

7. An implication of this—as discussed in chapter 4—is that during negotiation, states will overvalue concessions made to an adversary relative to the concessions granted to them by rivals. This suggests that the realist contention that successful cooperation requires that states receive "proportionate advantages in return" for concessions is misplaced (Grieco 1990, 47). Equal concessions leave both parties feeling a loss. From a realist's point of view, such a condition should never lead to cooperative outcomes.

NOTES FOR CHAPTER 6

1. The reasons for this are discussed below.

2. The brief description that follows reflects the decision making procedures for the community during the period of the Montreal Protocol negotiations. Obviously, these procedures continue to evolve and are quite different today. Additionally, while the EC was officially represented by the commission, national delegates also attended. The United States, unsure of the internal balance of power within the EC, feared that if member states were not direct signatories they might renege. Ultimately, it was agreed that only the EC was required to ratify an agreement.

3. Where the EC has no exclusive competence the member states act independently (Mastellone 1981).

4. The details and rationale behind such a mandate are discussed later.

5. The fact that the interests of Britain and France dominated the EC position is not contested in the literature on the Montreal Protocol. The purpose of this discussion is to unearth the institutional dynamics that permitted this condition, and establish the EC as a single decisionmaker with a single coherent policy for the purposes of this case.

6. For further discussion on the international consequences of U.S. action see Benedick 1991 (21–27) and Dotto and Schiff 1978 (148).

7. Indeed, the EC continued to extol its past actions protecting the ozone well into the negotiations (CEC 1986).

8. For further discussion of the early EC position see Szell 1985 and Guest 1985.

9. For a detailed presentation of European production, consumption and capacity statistics see CEC 1986.

10. The cost and comparative effectiveness of different control schemes was a central theme in the discussion leading up to the final agreement. For official summaries see United Nations Environmental Program, 1986, 1986a.

11. Such cost would of course be reduced further to the extent that the EC could negotiate a reduction short of a complete aerosol ban.

12. To be fair, Benedick seems to be suggesting, contra realism, that the loss of the aerosol propellants was too expensive to consider. However, the above described U.S. experience with an aerosol ban suggests that some other motivation is also possible.

13. Because the council had no intention of allowing the commission to negotiate earnestly on behalf of the EC, Commission representatives were unable to offer serious counterproposals in an attempt to secure relative gains over the United States. Realists have difficultly explaining such a policy of self-constraint that prevents states from pursuing relative gains.

14. Part of the U.S. proposal was that CFCs for aerosol use could not be produced for export. However, as noted above the growth sector in the industry was in nonaerosol uses like electronics, foam blowing, and packaging.

15. Clean Air Act § 157(b), 42 U.S.C. § 7457(b), 1982.

16. See for example *Stratospheric Ozone and Climate Protection Act,* S.571, 100th Congress, 1st session, 1987; *Stratospheric Protection Act of 1987,* S.570, 100th Congress, 1st session, 1987; *Stratospheric Ozone Protection Act of 1987,* HR.2036, 100th Congress, 1st Session, 1987; and *Ozone Protection and CFC Reduction Act of 1987,* HR. 2854, 100th Congress, 1st session, 1987.

17. A partial list of such goods included automobiles, refrigerators, air conditioners, packaging, insulation, Halon fire extinguishers, furniture, carpet, footwear, clothing, and electronics.

18. For an account of the evolution of scientific consensus on the harmful effects of CFCs see Roan 1989.

19. The report itself was entitled "NASA Atmospheric Ozone 1985." World Meteorological Organization Global Ozone Research and Monitoring Report, no. 16, 3 volumes (Geneva: World Meteorological Organization, 1986).

20. See for example EPA 1986.

21. See Roan 1989 for a detailed discussion.

22. See both Benedick 1991 (47–50) and Litfin 1992 (227–234).

23. In fact, U.S. producers strongly favored the EC position of a limited capacity cap. Such a cap would allow U.S. producers to continue at current levels of production. The U.S. proposal at the time called for reductions that the alliance actually opposed.

24. The alliance was actually strongly opposed to U.S. unilateral action.

25. It should be noted that this shift was not the result of compelling science, as the EC position on the validity of the scientific evidence had not changed. The French environmental minister, for example, continued to deny the link between CFCs and ozone depletion as late as March 1987.

26. For a discussion that develops the mathematical logic of different schemes, see Lammers 1988.

NOTES FOR CHAPTER 7

1. Often U.S. policy is incorrectly portrayed as one of gradually increasing support for a treaty. On those occasions when the break in U.S. policy is noted, it is not often placed in a larger theoretical context.

2. As discussed in chapter 2, this means that throughout this period the status quo and the reference point both represented current conditions.

3. The terms "technical" and "scientific" are here used interchangeably. By this I mean a focus on empirical questions like depletion rates, atmospheric modeling, ecological effects, chemical sinks, and so on. The distinction here is between issues that deal with physical dynamics of ozone layer depletion versus the economic impact of regulating CFCs.

4. At one early hearing, a committee chairman was reported to mutter, "This is pretty tough on a guy that never even had high school chemistry and has practiced law all his life." (Dotto and Schiff 1978, 193).

5. Several other major producers even offered their own versions of Dupont's pledge.

6. The most comprehensive discussion of the CFC industry's early efforts can be found in Dotto and Schiff 1978. See also Roan 1989.

7. Toward this end, Du Pont began publishing a series of flyers for wide dissemination, Kaiser Aluminum and Chemical Corporation published an "informational booklet," and industry scientists roamed the country challenging the validity of CFC science.

8. IMOS was sponsored by an impressive collection of federal agencies. These agencies included the Departments of Agriculture, Commerce, Defense, Health, Education and Welfare, Justice, State, and Transportation; the Consumer Product Safety Commission; Energy, Research and Administration; the Environmental Protection

Agency; the National Aeronautics and Space Administration; the National Science Foundation; and the Interdepartmental Committee for Atmospheric Sciences. Such broad participation meant that any conclusions reached in the final report represented a shared consensus within the federal government about the need for regulatory action.

9. The ban on aerosols did in fact have a significant short-term impact on global emission levels. But these gains were quickly overcome as other nonaerosol uses began to grow in importance.

10. Such information was not yet released to the public. U.S. regulatory agencies made public the decision and details for banning CFCs two weeks after they had disclosed this information to regulators from other countries at the international talks (Bastain 1982, 192).

11. At this time, Sweden, Norway, Canada and the Netherlands were each moving in some way to restrict domestic uses. But none of these were producing states and their share of the aerosol market was quite small. While lauded as progressive, that this constituted the totality of international reaction to the ozone threat was viewed as a failure by advocates for decisive international action.

12. As one member put it, "The witnesses have done a very effective job of marshaling the arguments in the testimony and putting it in proper perspective. As a result we can see not only the extensive effect of this potential regulation upon the economy in general, but also the impact on small business" (U.S. Congress 1981b).

13. See for example, Natural Resources Defense Council "Concerning the Impact of Policies to Protect the Ozone Layer on Small Business" in U.S. Congress 1981b, 192–196.

14. As noted previously, the CFC industry in the United States did eventually support an international agreement. Increasingly, U.S. producers faced a spate of local and state ballot initiatives intended to eliminate the use of CFCs. If continued, the result would be a national patchwork of legislation requiring different product standards across the country. While industry still viewed international cooperation on an ozone protocol as a significant gamble that might result in a comprehensive ban on CFCs, supporting a treaty offered the possibility of a single set of domestic standards. Domestic producers actually strongly favored the EC position of a limited capacity cap over the official U.S. position of an aerosol ban. Such a cap would allow U.S. producers to continue at current levels of production. As noted in chapter 6, U.S. delegates used this expression of support for an international agreement to bolster their negotiation position for cuts in production. Deliberately lost was the fact that American producers actually opposed that position.

15. The U.S. delegation was later forced to concede this point.

16. A mid-September deadline was established by the court for the publishing of an EPA protection plan.

17. Only after the Montreal agreement, and after objective empirical evidence of CFC damage was found, is it plausible to claim that ozone protection, to the extent that ecological collapse was a possibility, became a national security interest.

NOTES FOR CHAPTER 8

1. Initially, the protocol permitted exports to be subtracted from a state's allotted consumption. The provision was phased out over several years (Montreal Protocol on Substances that Deplete the Ozone Layer 1987).

2. This is of course not true for the United States, which exported little. Production was entirely consumed domestically.

3. On September 16, 1987, twenty-four nations signed the protocol. Several additional nations had made commitments to sign. Still, the majority of states had yet to make up their minds.

4. The emphasis on ecology at the expense of economics is common in discussions of the Montreal Protocol. See for example Hass 1992, Litfin 1994, Morrisette 1989, Parson 1992, and Cook 1990.

5. There never really was a "hole" over Antarctica. Rather, scientists observed a regular seasonal thinning of ozone over the polar ice cap during winter. With the arrival of warmer temperatures in the region, the localized thinning disappeared. A better analogy for the seasonal emergence of the ozone hole is one of a bucket of paint into which drops of thinner are dropped. Where the thinner hits, the paint is diluted. When stirred, the paint seems fine. However, after several such iterations the effects of the thinner render the paint so thin as to be useless.

6. Coordinated scientific study through the UNEP did continue, but this action was separate from the treaty discussions.

7. For a discussion, please see United Nations Environment Program 1989.

References

Abbott, Kenneth. 1999. International Relations Theory, International Law, and the Regime Governing Atrocities in Internal Conflicts. *American Journal of International Law* 93 (April): 361–369.

Alder, Emanuel. 1997. Seizing the Middle Ground: Constructivism in World Politics. *European Journal of International Relations* 3(3): 319–363.

Allision, Scott, and David Messick. 1985. The Group Attribution Error. *Journal of Experimental Social Psychology* 21(6): 563–579.

Akerlof, George. 2002 Behavioral Macroeconomics and Macroeconomic Behavior. *American Economic Review* 92(3): 411–432.

Argote, Linda, Mark Seabringt, and Linds Dyer. 1986. Individual Versus Group Use of Base-Rate and Individual Information. *Organizational Behavior and Human Decision Processes* 38(1): 65–75.

Axelrod, Robert M. 1984. *The Evolution of Cooperation.* New York: Basic Books.

Axelrod, Robert, and Robert Keohane. 1985. Achieving Cooperation Under Anarchy: Strategies and Institutions. *World Politics.* 38(October): 226–254.

Barkin, Samuel, and George Shambaugh. 1996. Common-Pool Resources and International Environmental Politics. *Environmental Politics* 5(3): 429–447.

Barnett, Richard. 1987. Testimony, House Committee on Energy and Commerce. *Ozone Layer Depletions.* Washington, D.C.: U.S. Government Printing Office.

Bastain, Carroll. 1982. The Formulation of Federal Policy. In *Stratospheric Ozone and Man,* edited by F. Bower and R. Ward. Boca Raton, Fla.: CRC Press.

Bell, David, Howard Raiffa, and Amos Tversky, eds. 1988. *Decision Making: Descriptive, Normative, and Prescriptive Interactions.* Cambridge, England: Cambridge University Press.

Benedick, Richard. 1987. Plenary Statement at Vienna, February 23, as reproduced in U.S. Congress, House Committee on Human Rights and International Organization, *U.S. Participation in International Organizations on Ozone Protocol,* Washington, D.C.: U.S. Government Printing Office.

———. 1987b. Plenary Statement at Vienna, February 23, as reproduced in U.S. House Committee on Foreign Affairs, *U.S. Participation in International Negotiations on the Ozone Protocol,* 100th cong., 1st session, March 1987.

———. 1991. *Ozone Diplomacy: New Directions in Safeguarding the Planet.* Cambridge: Harvard University Press.

Berejikian, Jeffrey. 1997. The Gains Debate: Framing State Choice. *American Political Science Review* 91(4): 789–805.

Berejikian, Jeffrey, and John Dryzek. 2000. Reflexive Action in International Politics. *British Journal of Political Science* 30(2): 193–216.

Berger, P. 1998. The Impact of Prospect Theory Based Framing Tactics on Advertising Effectiveness. *Omega-International Journal of Management Science* 26(5): 593–609.

Blanchard, Elwood. 1987. Testimony, House Committee on Energy and Commerce. *Ozone Layer Depletions.* Washingotn, D.C.: U.S. Government Printing Office.

Bleckman, Barry, and Stephen Kaplan. 1978. *Force Without War: U.S. Armed Forces as a Political Instrument.* Washington, D.C.: Brookings Institution.

Blum, Barbara. 1981. Prepared Statement at International meeting on Chlorofluoro-carbons. Oslo, Norway. As Reproduced in EPA Rulemaking on Chlorofluorocar-bons (CFCs).

Boettcher, William. 1995. Context, Numbers and Words. *Journal of Conflict Resolution* 39(3): 561–583.

Borges, B. 1998. Tests of Market Outcomes with Asymmetric Valuations of Gains and Losses: Smaller Gains, Fewer Trades, and Less value. *Journal of Economic Behavior and Organization* 33(2): 185–193.

Bottom, W.P. 1998. Negotiator Risk: Sources of Uncertainty and the Impact of Reference Points on Negotiated Agreements. *Organizational Behavior and Human Decision Processes* 76(2): 89–112.

Brewer, Marilyn, and Roderick Kramer. 1986. Choice Behavior in Social Dilemmas: Effects of Social Identity, Group Size and Decision Framing. *Journal of Personality and Social Psychology,* 50, 543–549.

Budescu, D., S. Weinberg, and T. Wallsten. 1988. Decisions Based on Numerically and Verbally Expressed Uncertainties. *Journal of Experimental Psychology* 14(2): 281–294.

Bueno de Mesquita, Bruce. 2000. *Principles of International Politics: People's Power, Preferences, and Perceptions.* Washington D.C.: CQ Press.

Cameron, M. A. 1997. North-American Free-Trade Negotiations: Liberalization Games Between Asymmetric Players. *European Journal of International Relations* 3(1): 105–140.

Checkel, Jeffrey. 1998. The Constructivist Turn in International Relations Theory. *World Politics* 50 (Jan.): 324–348.

Clean Air Act. 1982. Public Law 95. As amended.

Commission of the European Communities (CEC). 1985. *Chlorofluorocarbons in the Environment: Updating the Situation, at Brussels.* Brussels: Commission of the European Communities.

———. 1986. *Chlorofluorocarbons in the Environment: A Reexamination of Control Measures.* Brussels: Commission of the European Communities.

Congressional Record. 1987. 100th Cong., 1st sess. Vol. 133, No. 25.

Cook, Elizabeth. 1990. Global Environmental Advocacy: Citizen Activism in Protecting the Ozone Layer. *AMBIO* 19(summer): 334–338.

Cosmides, Leda. 1989. The Logic of Social Exchange: Has Natural Selection Shaped how Humans Reason? Studies with the Watson Selection Task. *Cognition* 31(3): 187–276.

Costello, M. 1996. Impure Public Goods, Relative Gains, and International Cooperation. *Policy Studies Journal* 24(4): 578–594.

Council on Environmental Quality and Federal Council for Science and Technology (CEQ). 1974. *Fluorocarbons and the Environment.* Washington, D.C.: U.S. Government Printing Office.

Dawes, Robyn. 1988. *Rational Choice in an Uncertain World.* Chicago: Harcort, Brace, Jovanovich.

Dedreu, Carston, and Christopher McCusker. 1997. Gain-Loss Frames and Cooperation in 2-Person Social Dilemmas: A Transformational Analysis. *Journal of Personality and Social Psychology* 72(5): 1093–1106.

Donniger, David. 1988. Politics of the Ozone Layer. *Issues in Science and Technology* 4(3): 86–92.

Doolittle, Diane. 1989. Underestimating Ozone Depletion: The Meandering Road to the Montreal Protocol. *Ecology and Law Quarterly* 16(4): 407–441.

Dotto, Lydo, and Harold Schiff. 1978. *The Ozone War.* Garden City, N.Y.: Doubleday.

Economist. 1999. Rethinking Thinking. Editorial, December 18–24.

Elliott, Kimberly. 1998. The Sanctions Glass: Half Full or Completely Empty. *International Security* 23 (summer): 50–65.

Environmental Protection Agency (EPA). 1986. *Environmental Protection Agency and United Nations Environmental Program Effects of Changes in Stratospheric Ozone and Global Climate Change.* Washington, D.C.: Environmental Protection Agency.

Erve, I., and B Cohen. 1990. Verbal Versus Numerical Probability: Efficiency, Biases, and the Preference Paradox. *Organizational Behavior and Human Decision Processes* 45: 1–18.

Evans, Peter. 1993. Building an Integrative Approach to International and Domestic Politics: Reflections and Projections in *Double Edged Diplomacy,* edited by Peter Evans, Harold Jacobson, and Robert Putnam. Berkeley: University of California Press.

Farnham, Barbara. 1992. Roosevelt and the Munich Crisis: Insights from Prospect Theory. *Political Psychology* 13(2): 205–235.

Faucheux, Sylvie, and J.-F. Noel. 1988. *Did the Ozone War End in Montreal?* Paris: Université de Paris, Center of Économie-Espace-Environment.

Fearon, James. 1997. Signaling Foreign Policy Interests: Tying Hands versus sinking Costs. *Journal of Conflict Resolution* 41(1): 68–90.

Frey, Bruno, and Renier Eichenberger. 1989. Should Social Scientists Care about Choice Anomalies? *Rationality and Society* 1(1): 101–122.

Friedman, Milton. 1953. *Essays in Positive Economics.* Chicago: University of Chicago Press.

Geva, Nehmia, and Alex Minz, eds. 1997. *Decision making on War and Peace: The Cognitive-Rational Debate.* Boulder, Colo.: Lynne Reinner Publishers.

Gilpin, Robert. 1981. War and Change in World Politics. Cambridge, N.Y.: Cambridge University Press.

———. 1987. *Political Economy of International Relations.* Princeton, N.J.: Princeton University Press.

Grether, D.M., and C.R. Plott. 1979. The Economic Theory of Choice and the Preference Reversal Phenomenon. *American Economic Review* 69(4): 623–638.

Grieco, Joseph M. 1988. Anarchy and the Limits of Cooperation. *International Organization* 42(3): 485–507.

———. 1990. *Cooperation Among Nations: Europe, America, and Non-tariff Barriers to Trade.* Cornell Studies in Political Economy. Ithaca, N.Y.: Cornell University Press.

———. 1993. Comment. *American Political Science Review* 87 (September): 729–735.

Guest, I. 1985. U.S. and E.C. Split on Danger to Ozone. *International Herald Tribune.* 29 January.

Haaga, Kohler. 1987. *Projections of Consumption of Products Using Chlorofluorocarbons in Developing Countries.* Santa Monica: Rand Corporation.

Haass, Richard. 1997. Sanctioning Madness. *Foreign Affairs* 76(6): 74–85.

Haigh, Nigel. 1991. The European Community and International Environmental Policy. *International Environmental Affairs* 3(3): 163–180.

Haskel, Barbara. 1974. Disparities, Strategies, and Opportunity Costs: The Examination of Scandinavian Economic Market Negotiations. *International Studies Quarterly* 18(1): 3–30.

Hass, Peter. 1992. Banning Chlorofluorocarbons: Epistemic Community Attempts to Protect the Stratospheric Ozone. *International Organization* 46(1): 187–224.

Herman, R.K., P.E. Tetlock, and M.N. Diascro. 2001. How Americans Think about Trade: Reconciling Conflicts among Money, Power, and Principles. *International Studies Quarterly* 45(2): 191–218.

Hopmann, Terrence. 1995. Two Paradigms of negotiation: Bargaining and Problem Solving. *Annals of the American Academy of Political and Social Science* 542 (Nov.): 24–48.

Jachtenfuchs, Markus. 1990. The European Community and the Protection of the Ozone Layer. *Journal of Common Market Studies* 3 (March): 261–277.

Janus, Irving. 1982. *Groupthink: Psychological Studies of Policy Decisions and Fiascoes.* 2nd ed. Boston: Houghton Mifflin.

Jervis, Robert. 1978. Realism, Game Theory, and Cooperation. *World Politics* 30 (January): 317–349.

———. 1988. Realism, Game Theory, and Cooperation. *World Politics* 40 (April): 317–349.

———. 1992. The Political Implications of Loss Aversion. *Political Psychology* 13(2): 187–204.

———. 1999. Realism, Neoliberalism, and Cooperation—Understanding the Debate. *International Security* 24(1): 42–63.

Jones, Bryan D. 1999. Bounded Rationality. *Annual Review of Political Science* 2: 297–321.

Kaempfer, William, and Anton Lowenberg. 1999. Unilateral Versus Multilateral International Sanctions: A Public Choice Perspective. *International Studies Quarterly* 43(1): 37–58.

Kahneman, Daniel, and Amos Tversky. 1979. Prospect Theory: An Analysis of Decisions Under Risk. *Econometrica* 47(2): 263–291.

———. 1982. The Psychology of Preferences. Scientific American 246(1): 160–173.

———. 1990. Prospect Theory: An Analysis of Decision Under Risk. In *Rationality in Action: Contemporary Approaches,* edited by P. Moser. New York: Cambridge University Press.

Kahneman, Daniel, Paul Slovic, and Amos Tversky, eds. 1982. *Judgment Under Uncertainty: Heuristics and Biases.* Cambridge, England: Cambridge University Press.

Kegley, Charles, and Gregory Raymond. 1994. *A Multipolar Peace? Great-Power Politics in the Twenty-First Century.* New York: St. Martin's Press.

Keohane, Robert. 1983. The Demand for International Regimes. In *International Regimes,* edited by S. Krasner. Ithaca, N.Y.: Cornell University Press.

———. 1984. *After Hegemony: Cooperation and Discord in the World Political Economy.* Princeton, N.J.: Princeton University Press.

Krasner, Stephen, ed. 1983. *International Regimes.* Ithaca, N.Y.: Cornell University Press.

———. 1991. Global Communications and National Power: Life on the Pareto Frontier. *World Politics* 43(April): 336–366.

Kristensen, H. 1997. Adoption of Cognitive Reference Points in Negotiations. *Acta Psychologica* 97(3): 277–288.

Kuhberger, A. 1995. The Framing of Decisions: A New Look at Old Problems. *Organizational Behavior and Human Decision Processes* 62: 230–240.

Kydd, Andrew, and Duncan Snidal. 1993. Progress in Game-Theoretic Analysis of International Regimes. In *Regime Theory and International Relations,* edited by V. Rittberger. Oxford: Clarendon Press.

Laibson, D. 1998. Amos Tversky and the Ascent of Behavorial Economics. *Journal of Risk and Uncertainty* 16(1): 7–47.

Lammers, Johan. 1988. Efforts to Develop a Protocol on Chlorofluorocarbons to the Vienna Convention for the Protection of the Ozone Layer. *Hague Yearbook of International Law* 1 (winter): 225–269.

Lebow, Richard Ned, and Janice Gross Stein. 1987. Beyond Deterrence. *Journal of Social Issues* 43(4): 5–71.

Lee, D. 1994. The Impact of Firms' Risk-Taking Attitudes on Advertising Budgets. *Journal of Business Research* 31(2–3): 247–256.

Levy, Jack. 1992. Prospect Theory and International Relations: Theoretical Applications and Analytical Problems. *Political Psychology* 13(2): 283–310.

———. 1996. Crisis, Conflict and War. *International Political Science Review* 17(2): 179–195.

———. 1996. Loss Aversion, Framing, and Bargaining: The Implications of Prospect Theory for International Conflict. *International Political Science Review* 17(2): 179–195.

———. 1997. Prospect Theory, Rational Choice, and International Relations Theory. *International Studies Quarterly* 41(1): 87–112.

Lindsday, James. 1986. Trade Sanctions as Policy Instruments: A Re-examination. *International Studies Quarterly* 30(2): 153–174.

Litfin, Karen. 1992. Power and Knowledge in International Environmental Politics: The Case of Ozone Depletion. Ph.D. dissertation, University of California at Los Angeles.

———. 1994. Ozone Discourses: Science and Politics in Global Environmental Cooperation. New York: Columbia University Press.

Maddox, John. 1987. The Great Ozone Controversy. *Nature* 329 (September): 101.

Marriot, V.J. 1975. Testimony, Committee on Aeronautical and Space Sciences. *Stratospheric Ozone Depletion.* Washington, D.C.: U.S. Government Printing Office.

Mastanduno, Michael. 1991. Do Relative Gains Matter? America's Response to Japanese Industrial Policy. *International Security* 16(1): 73–113.

———. 1993. Framing the Japan Problem: The Bush Administration and the Structural Impediments Initiative. In *Choosing to Cooperate: How States Avoid Loss,* edited by J. Stien and L. Pauly. Baltimore: Johns Hopkins University Press.

Mastellone, Carlo. 1981. The External Relations of the EEC in the Field of Environmental Protection. *International and Comparative Law Quarterly* 23(1): 105–117.

Mayer, Fredrick. 1992. Managing Domestic Differences in International Negotiations: The Strategic Use of Side Payments. *International Organization* 46(4): 793–818.

McDermott, Rose. 1992. Prospect Theory in International Relations: The Iranian Hostage Rescue Mission. *Political Psychology* 13(2): 237–263.

———. 1998. *Risk-taking in International Politics: Prospect Theory in American Foreign Policy.* Ann Arbor: University of Michigan Press.

McInerney, Audry. 1992. Prospect Theory and Soviet Policy Towards Syria, 1966–1967. *Political Psychology* 13(2): 265–282.

Milner, Helen. 1991. The Assumption of Anarchy in International Relations Theory: A Critique. *Review of International Studies* 17 (January): 67–85.

Mitchell, Ronald. 1994. Regime Design Matters: Intentional Oil Pollution and Treaty Compliance. *International Organization* 48 (Summer): 425–458.

Moravcsic, Andrew. 1993. Integrating International and Domestic Theories of International Bargaining. *Double-Edged Diplomacy,* edited by Peter Evans, Harold Jacobson, and Robert Putnam. Berkley: University of California Press.

Morganthau, Hans. 1960. *Politics Among Nations: The Struggle for Power and Peace.* 6th ed. New York: Alfred A. Knopf.

Morrisette, Peter. 1989. The Evolution of Policy Responses to Stratospheric Ozone Depletion. *Natural Resources Journal* 29 (summer): 793–820.

Mowen, John, and James Gentry. 1980. Investigation of the Preference-Reversal Phenomenon in a New Product Introduction Task. *Journal of Applied Psychology* 65 (December): 715–722.

Mulford, Mathew, and Jeffrey Berejikian. 2002. Behavioural Decision Theory and the Gains Debate in International Politics. *Political Studies* 50(2): 209–229.

Munasinghe, Mohan, and Kenneth King. 1991. *Issues and Options in Implementing the Montreal Protocol in Developing Countries.* Nairobi: World Bank, Environment Department.

Myers, D., and H. Lamm. 1976. Group Polarization Phenomena. *Psychological Bulletin* 83(1): 602–627.

Nalebuff, Barry. 1991. Rational Deterrence in an Imperfect World. *World Politics* 43 (April): 313–335.

Nichols, P. 1996. Realism, Liberalism, Values and the World Trade Organization. *University of Pennsylvania Journal of International Economic Law* 17(3): 851–882.

Nincic, Miroslav. 1997. Loss Aversion and the Domestic Context of Military Intervention. *Political Research Quarterly* 50(1): 97–120.

Nincic, Miroslav, and Peter Wallensteen. 1983. Economic Coercion and Foreign Policy. In *Dilemmas of Economic Coercion: Sanctions in World Politics,* edited by M. Nincic and P. Wallensteen. New York: Prager.

Ostrom, Elinor. 1998. A Behavioral Approach to the Rational Choice Theory of Collective Action. *American Political Science Review* 92(1): 1–22.

Pape, Robert. 1997. Why Economic Sanctions do not Work. *International Security* 22 (fall): 90–136.

Parson, Edward. 1992. *Protecting the Ozone layer: The Evolution and Impact of International Institutions.* Boston: John F. Kennedy School of Government.

Pauly, Louis. 1993. The Political Foundations of Multilateral Economic Surveillance. In *Choosing to Cooperate: How States Avoid War,* edited by J. Stein and L. Pauly. Baltimore: Johns Hopkins University Press.

Petrakis, E. 1996. Environmental Consciousness and Moral Hazard in International Agreements to Protect the Environment. *Journal of Public Economics* 60(1): 95–110.

Plous, Scott. 1993. *The Psychology of Judgment and Decision Making.* Philadelphia: Temple University Press.

Powell, Robert. 1991. Absolute and Relative Gains in International Relations Theory. *American Political Science Review* 85(4): 1303–1320.

———. 1993. Response. *American Political Science Review* 87 (September): 735–737.

———. 1994. Anarchy in International Relations Theory: The Neorealist-Neoliberal Debate. *International Organization* 42(2): 313–344.

Putnam, Robert. 1988. Diplomacy and Domestic Politics: The Logic of Two-Level Games. *International Organization* 42 (summer): 427–460.

Quatrone, George, and Amos Tversky. 1988. Contrasting Rational and Psychological Analyses of Political Choice. *American Political Science Review* 82 (September): 23–36.

Reyna, Valerie, and Charles Brainerd. 1991. Fuzzy-Trace Theory and Framing Effects in Choice: Grist Extraction, Truncation and Conversion. *Journal of Behavioral Decision Making* 4: 249–262.

Richardson, Louis. 1993. Avoiding and Incurring Losses: Decision-Making in the Suez Crisis. In *Choosing to Cooperate: How States Avoid Loss,* edited by J. Stein and L. Pauly. Baltimore: Johns Hopkins University Press.

Roan, Sharon. 1989. *Ozone Crisis: The 15-year Evolution of a Sudden Emergency.* New York: John Wiley.

Rosati, Jerel. 2001. The Power of human Cognition in the Study of World Politics. *International Studies Review* 2(3): 45–75.

Rothman, Alexander, and Peter Slovey. 1997. Shaping Perceptions to Motivate Healthy Behavior: The Role of Message Framing. *Psychological Bulletin* 121(1): 3–19.

Russell, Thomas, and Richard Thaler. 1985. The Relevance of Quasi-Rationality in Competitive Markets. *American Economic Review* 75 (December): 1071–1082.

Sand, Peter. 1985. Protecting the Ozone Layer: The Vienna Convention is Adopted. *Environment* 27(5): 19–43.

Schaubroeck, John. 1994. Prospect Theory Predictions When Escalation is Not the Only Chance to Recover Sunk Costs. *Organizational Behavior and Human Decision Processes* 51(1): 59–82.

Schmidt, Brian. 1998. *The Political Discourse of Anarchy: A Disciplinary History of International Relations.* Albany: State University of New York Press.

Schoemaker, Paul. 1982. The Expected Utility Model: Its Variants, Purposes, Evidence and Limitations. *Journal of Economic Literature* 20(2): 529–563.

Sell, Jane, and Yeongi Son. 1997. Comparing Public Goods with Common Pool Resources: Three Experiments. *Social Psychology Quarterly* 60(2): 118–137.

Shafir, Eldar. 1992. Prospect Theory and Political Analysis: A Psychological Perspective. *Political Psychology* 13(2): 311–322.

Simon, Herbert Alexander. 1983. *Reason in Human Affairs.* Harry Camp lectures at Stanford University, 1982. Stanford, Calif.: Stanford University Press.

Simon, Herbert. 1985. Human nature in Politics: the Dialogue of Psychology with Political Science. *American Political Science Review* 79(2): 293–304.

Sinjders, Chris, and Werner Raub. 1998. Revolution and Risk: Paradoxical Consequences of Risk Aversion in Interdependent Situations. *Rationality and Society* 10(4): 405–425.

Snidal, Duncan. 1991. Relative Gains and the Pattern of International Cooperation. *American Political Science Review* 85(3): 701–725.

———. 1993a. The Relative Gains Problem for International Cooperation: Response to Grieco. *American Political Science Review* 87(3): 738–742.

———. 1993b. Response. *American Political Science Review* 87 (September): 738–742.

Stein, Arthur. 1983. Coordination and Collaboration: Regimes in an Anarchic World. In *International Regimes,* edited by S. Krasner. Ithaca, N.Y. and London: Cornell University Press.

———. 1990. *Why Nations Cooperate: Circumstance and Choice in International Relations.* Ithaca, N.Y. and London: Cornell University Press.

Stein, Janice. 1989. Getting to the Table: The Triggers, Stages, Function, and Consequences of Prenegotiation. In *Getting to the Table: The Processes of International Prenegotiation,* edited by J. Stein. Baltimore: Johns Hopkins University Press.

Stein, Janice, and Louis Pauly, eds. 1993. *Choosing to Cooperate: How States Avoid Loss.* Baltimore: Johns Hopkins University Press.

Steinbruner, John. 1976. Beyond Rational Deterrence: The Struggle for New Conceptions. *World Politics* 28(2): 223–245.

Szell, Patrick. 1985. The Vienna Convention for the Protection of the Ozone Layer. *International Digest of Health Legislation* 36(3): 839–842.

't Hart, Paul, Eric Stern, and Bengt Sundelius, eds. 1997. *Beyond Groupthink: Political Group Dynamics and Foreign Policy-Making.* Ann Arbor: University of Michigan Press.

Taylor, M. Scott. 1994. Once-Off and Continuing Gains from Trade. *Review of Economic Studies* 61(3): 589–601.

Thomas, Lee. 1987. Testimony Before Congress. In U.S. Congress. 1987. House Committee on Energy and Commerce. *Ozone Layer Depletions*. Washington, D.C.: U.S. Government Printing.

Tversky, Amos, and Daniel Kahneman. 1981. The Framing of Decisions and the Psychology of Choice. *Science* 211 (January 30): 453–458.

———. 1986. Rational Choice and the Framing of Decisions. *Journal of Business* 59(4): 251–278.

Tversky, Amos, Paul Slovic, and Daniel Kahneman. 1990. The Causes of Preference Reversal. *American Economic Review* 80(1): 204–217.

United Nations Environmental Program. 1986. Doc#. UNEP/WG/148/2.

———. 1986a. Doc#. UNEP/WG/148/3.

———. 1989. Doc#. UNEP/OzL.Pro.WGII(1) /4.

U.S. Department of State. 1985. *Protecting the Ozone Layer*. Washington D.C.: United States Department of State.

———. 1986. *Principles for an International Protocol on Stratospheric Ozone Protection*. Mimeograph, November 3.

van Assen, Malm. 1990. Effects of Individual Decision Theory Assumptions on Predicitions of Cooperation in Social Dilemmas. *Journal of Mathematical Sociology* 23(2): 143–153.

Van Dijk and Henk Wilke. 1995. Coordination Rules in Asymetric Social Dilemmas: A Comparison between Public Good Dilemmas and Resource Dilemmas. *Journal of Experimental Social Psychology* 31: 1–27.

Vasquez, John A. 1998. *The Power of Power Politics: From Classical Realism to Neotraditionalism*. Cambridge: Cambridge University Press.

Vertzberger, Yaacov. 1990. *The World in their Minds*. Stanford: Stanford University Press.

von Newman, John, and Oskar Morgenstern. 1947. *Theory of Games and Economic Behavior*. Princeton: Princeton University Press.

Walt, Stephen. 1998. International Relations: One World, Many Theories. *Foreign Policy* 110 (spring): 29–47.

Waltz, Kenneth. 1979. *Theory of International Politics*. Reading, Mass.: Addison-Wesley.

Waltz, Kenneth. 1990. Realist Thought and Neorealist Theory. *Journal of International Affairs* 44(1): 21–37.

Welch, David. 1993. The Politics and Psychology of Restraint: Israeli Decision-Making in the Gulf War. In *Choosing to Cooperate: How States Avoid War*, edited by J. Stein and L. Pauly. Baltimore: Johns Hopkins University Press.

Wendt, Alexander. 1992. Anarchy Is What States Make of It: The Social Construction of Power Politics. *International Organization* 46 (spring): 391–425.

Wettstad, Jorgen. 1999. *Designing Effective Environmental Regimes: The Key Conditions.* Cheltenham, England: Edward Elgar.

Weyland, Kurt. 1996. Risk Taking in Latin American Economic Restructuring: Lessons from Prospect Theory. *International Studies Quarterly* 40(2): 185–208.

———. 1998. Swallowing the Bitter Pill: Sources of Popular Support for Neoliberal Reform in Latin America. *Comparative Political Studies* 31(5): 539–568.

White, Glen. 1993. Escalating Commitment in Individual and Group Decision Making: A Prospect Theory Approach. *Organizational Behavior and Human Decision Making Processes* 54(3): 430–455.

Whyte, Glen. 1998. Recasting Janis's Groupthink Model: The Key Role of Collective Decision Fiascoes. *Organizational Behavior and Human Decision Making Processes* 73(2–3): 185–209.

Wirth, David. 1987. Testimony, House Committee on Energy and Commerce. *Ozone Layer Depletions.* Washington, D.C.: U.S. Government Printing Office.

Wright, William, and Urton Anderson. 1989. Effects of Situation Familiarity and Financial Incentives on the Use of Anchoring and Adjustment Heuristics for Probability Assessment. *Organizational Behavior and Human Decision Making Processes* 44 (August): 68–82.

Yaniv, G. 1999. Tax Compliance and Advance Tax Payments: A Prospect Theory Analysis. *National Tax Journal* 52(4): 753–764.

Zagare, Frank. 1990. Rationality and Deterrence. *World Politics* 42(2): 238–260.

List of Titles in the
SUNY series in Global Politics

American Patriotism in a Global Society – Betty Jean Craige

The Political Discourse of Anarchy: A Disciplinary History of International Relations – Brian C. Schmidt

From Pirates to Drug Lords: The Post – Cold War Caribbean Security Environment – Michael C. Desch, Jorge I. Dominguez, and Andres Serbin (eds.)

Collective Conflict Management and Changing World Politics – Joseph Lepgold and Thomas G. Weiss (eds.)

Zones of Peace in the Third World: South America and West Africa in Comparative Perspective – Arie M. Kacowicz

Private Authority and International Affairs – A. Claire Cutler, Virginia Haufler, and Tony Porter (eds.)

Harmonizing Europe: Nation-States within the Common Market – Francesco G. Duina

Economic Interdependence in Ukrainian-Russian Relations – Paul J. D'Anieri

Leapfrogging Development? The Political Economy of Telecommunications Restructuring – J. P. Singh

States, Firms, and Power: Successful Sanctions in United States Foreign Policy – George E. Shambaugh

Approaches to Global Governance Theory – Martin Hewson and Timothy J. Sinclair (eds.)

After Authority: War, Peace, and Global Politics in the Twenty-First Century – Ronnie D. Lipschutz

Pondering Postinternationalism: A Paradigm for the Twenty-First Century? – Heidi H. Hobbs (ed.)

Beyond Boundaries? Disciplines, Paradigms, and Theoretical Integration in International Studies – Rudra Sil and Eileen M. Doherty (eds.)

Why Movements Matter: The West German Peace Movement and U. S. Arms Control Policy – Steve Breyman

145

International Relations – Still an American Social Science? Toward Diversity in International Thought – Robert M. A. Crawford and Darryl S. L. Jarvis (eds.)

Which Lessons Matter? American Foreign Policy Decision Making in the Middle East, 1979 – 1987 – Christopher Hemmer (ed.)

Hierarchy Amidst Anarchy: Transaction Costs and Institutional Choice – Katja Weber

Counter-Hegemony and Foreign Policy: The Dialectics of Marginalized and Global Forces in Jamaica – Randolph B. Persaud

Global Limits: Immanuel Kant, International Relations, and Critique of World Politics – Mark F. N. Franke

Power and Ideas: North-South Politics of Intellectual Property and Antitrust – Susan K. Sell

Money and Power in Europe: The Political Economy of European Monetary Cooperation – Matthias Kaelberer

Agency and Ethics: The Politics of Military Intervention – Anthony F. Lang, Jr.

Life After the Soviet Union: The Newly Independent Republics of the Transcaucasus and Central Asia – Nozar Alaolmolki

Theories of International Cooperation and the Primacy of Anarchy: Explaining U. S. International Monetary Policy-Making After Bretton Woods – Jennifer Sterling-Folker

Information Technologies and Global Politics: The Changing Scope of Power and Governance – James N. Rosenau and J. P. Singh (eds.)

Technology, Democracy, and Development: International Conflict and Cooperation in the Information Age – Juliann Emmons Allison (ed.)

The Arab-Israeli Conflict Transformed: Fifty Years of Interstate and Ethnic Crises—Hemda Ben-Yehuda and Shmuel Sandler

Systems of Violence: The Political Economy of War and Peace in Colombia – Nazih Richani

Debating the Global Financial Architecture – Leslie Elliot Armijo

Political Space: Frontiers of Change and Governance in a Globalizing World – Yale Ferguson and R. J. Barry Jones (eds.)

Crisis Theory and World Order: Heideggerian Reflections – Norman K. Swazo

Political Identity and Social Change: The Remaking of the South African Social Order – Jamie Frueh

Social Construction and the Logic of Money: Financial Predominance and International Economic Leadership – J. Samuel Barkin

What Moves Man: The Realist Theory of International Relations and Its Judgment of Human Nature – Annette Freyberg-Inan

Democratizing Global Politics: Discourse Norms, International Regimes, and Political Community – Rodger A. Payne and Nayef H. Samhat

Index